Twin Falls Centurybook

1904–2004

Mary J. Inman

Illustrated by Mary J. Inman

Hosteler Press
Twin Falls, Idaho
2003

Printed in the United States of America
06 05 04 03 5 4 3 2
ISBN 0-9676981-5-4

Other Works by Mary J. Inman

Available at Barnes and Noble, Waldenbooks, and at visitor centers and gift shops in Twin Falls, Idaho, and along the Oregon Trail, or write to Mary J. Inman, 434 Taylor Street, Twin Falls, Idaho 83301.

On CD:

- *Living History Stories of the Oregon Trail*, Vol. I
  "Oregon Bound 1843"
  "Trailblazers of the Oregon Trail"
- *Living History Stories of the Oregon Trail*, Vol. II
  "Oregon Bound 1852"
  "Indians Along the Oregon Trail"

On tape cassette:

- *Twin Falls Historical Tours*, Vol. I
  "Pre–Twin Falls History," auto tour
  "Twin Falls Townsite, 1904," walking tour
- *Twin Falls Historical Tours*, Vol. II
  "The Irrigation Story," auto tour
  "Twin Falls Village, 1905–06," walking tour

Illustrations

Illustrations in this book are the author's interpretations of photographs or artwork from the following sources: Howard Allen's 1970s Twin Falls calendars, *Audubon*, Clarence Bisbee, Chris Bolton, Andrew Crane, East Coast Migrant Stream Foundation, Frank Florence, Idaho State Historical Society, Ron James: *Ruins of a World*, Oliver Johnson, Frank McCarthy: *Drive to the Buffalo Jump*, *National Parks*, Dan Obenchain, Phyllis Perrine, *The Post Register*, Pearl M. Rayl, Einar Sande, Zoe Ann Schaub, Howard Terpning: *The Feast*, *The Times-News*, Twin Falls Area Chamber of Commerce, Twin Falls County Historical Society, Twin Falls League of Women Voters, Twin Falls Public Library.

Book Design

by Rose Garber, Aspen Design, Twin Falls, Idaho

Contents

Underwritten by
Grace Smith and Kenneth A. Keveren Foundation

Providing copies of this book to the
Twin Falls District Schools are donations from
D. L. Evans Bank
Optimists Club of Twin Falls
Kiwanis Club of Twin Falls
Blue Lakes Rotary Club of Twin Falls

Acknowledgments

Late in 1997, the Twin Falls City Council asked for volunteers to serve on a Centennial Committee to plan the city's one hundredth birthday celebration in 2004. I volunteered and began reading up on the town's history. When I read Donna Scott's book that was published for the Idaho State Centennial in 1990—*Tribute to the Past, Legacy for the Future*, a collection of stories of early Twin Falls settlers—I found it awesome. Here was the "heart and soul" of a town just waiting for "flesh and bones" so it could walk into its centennial celebration and on into the next century. I had to write this book, using Donna's stories as the basis. In the Twin Falls Public Library I made another discovery just as exciting: a collection of stories written by students in Virginia Ricketts's adult education classes at the College of Southern Idaho. Here were the "flesh and bones."

From both references I took stories and used as many quotes as possible in order to cite the sources. Stories that I used but did not quote are from Jerry A. Davis, Pauline F. Harvey, Shauna Robinson, Vesta Mayland, Lorraine Creasy, Duane Ramseyer, Frances Harris, Barbara A. McKain, Francis Johnson, Roxie Simcoe, Raye Warren, Mary Lou Christiansen, Mark Jones, Ethel Piland, Mary Modeen, Fay Parrott, Anna Davis, Emma Wells, Irvin Ehlers, Beverly Nelson, Mary Ann Sweet. I am also indebted to *The Times-News* for the current stories they published since 1998 that I used to bring this history up to 2004.

At the end of the first four chapters under Suggested Reading you will find listed many of the other references and sources I used, most of them found in the Twin Falls Public Library, on the Idaho shelf or in the Idaho Room. Everyone I interviewed gave me stories, and most of them are quoted and cited to make this history of Twin Falls the story of the people who lived it. I know I missed many good stories of many good people, events, and projects, and I know I will hear about it—then one day I will have to write a *Son of Centurybook*.

A heart-felt thanks goes to all who helped and encouraged me, especially Jay Goemmer, Donna Scott, Phyllis Perrine, Mary Alice Florence, Fred Sanger, Emery Petersen, Marge Slotten, and David Mead.

I hope you enjoy reading this book as much as I enjoyed writing it.

—Mary

Chapter 1

Pre–Twin Falls History

A High Desert Plain Was Formed

Fifteen million years ago, the "hot spot" that today fuels the geysers of Yellowstone National Park was under Craters of the Moon National Monument near Arco, Idaho. While the drifting continental plate lingered there, pressure from the hot spot caused a region of uplift followed by cataclysmic volcanic eruptions. When the pressure abated, the earth broke open to a long, 62-mile gash of fissure vents, now called the Great Rift. The lava that flowed quietly from the Rift's shield volcanoes buried the calderas left by the earlier volcanoes; when gasses were present, spatter cones and cinder cones developed. Over the millennia, these successive lava flows alternated with glacier-laid sedimentation to form the 30,000-square-mile volcanic scar, now called the Snake River Plain, and to push that mighty river's course into a great crescent arc.

A mere fifteen thousand years ago, Lake Bonneville, which covered much of Utah, broke through its northern rim releasing the pent-up power of its wall of water. The unimaginable violence of the Bonneville Flood scoured the Snake River Canyon as it cut through the layers of lava and sediment in its rush to the Columbia River. The resulting gradient of the Snake River through this spectacular canyon—fifty miles long and five hundred feet deep in places—gave the river's water the potential power to bring lush life to the arid desert. In this desert, where the Snake River makes its most southerly sweep, the townsite of Twin Falls would be established on the canyon's south side in 1904.

Originating in the South Hills ten miles south of the townsite are two creeks that continue to augment the flow of the Snake River. Dry Creek flows into the river near Star Falls, which is thirty miles east of the townsite and below the cataract called Cauldron Linn. Down canyon and two miles west of the townsite, Rock Creek joins the Snake just below Auger Falls. The tract of land watered by those two creeks, measuring roughly ten miles long by thirty-two miles wide, is the area covered in this pre–Twin Falls History and will be referred to as Twin Falls.

Many People Passed Through

There was magic in the Magic Valley long before white man came. The rivers were clean and running free. The air was clean, and at night the stars put on a show for free. Salmon and sturgeon were the kings and queens of the river. Piñon nuts to the south, camas bulbs to the north, and in between abundant wildlife and hot springs.

—Bill Chisholm, Buhl activist (1999)

Indians—Shoshone, Bannock, Paiute—hunted, gathered, fished, and camped along these waters for countless generations before the first white men came down the Snake River in 1811. Led by Wilson Price Hunt, the overland group of John Jacob Astor's Pacific Fur Company suffered a drowning at the rapids that the Scotsman Donald McKenzie named Cauldron Linn (boiling pot). There they were forced to abandon their canoes and the river. McKenzie and eighteen men scrambled to the north side; Hunt with forty men struggled to the Twin Falls side of the river for a grueling, uncharted trek on foot to the Columbia River.

McKenzie arrived first at Fort Astoria, already established at the mouth of the Columbia by the men Astor had sent by sea. The British Northwest Fur Company quickly went to the area from the British Territory of Canada and set up trading posts among the Northwest Indian tribes in competition with the Astorians. Hunt and his men arrived at Fort Astoria in mid-February 1812.

In June a party led by Robert Stuart left Astoria taking dispatches to Mr. Astor who, having lost two supply ships at sea, heard nothing of his enterprise for almost two years. Stuart's 7-man party passed through Twin Falls on horseback, retracing Hunt's route. (Robert Stuart Junior High School was named in honor of Twin Falls's early visitor.) Before reaching St. Louis, Stuart learned that the United States and Great Britain were at war—the War of 1812. The British took Fort Astoria and expelled the Americans from Oregon.

For the next decade, the British Northwest Fur Company dominated Oregon country from the Pacific Ocean to the Rocky Mountains. Astoria was renamed Fort George and made headquarters. From there, brigades led by Donald McKenzie (who changed company loyalty—again), Alexander Ross, and Peter Skene Ogden supplied the company's trading posts in exchange for furs. Their Shoshone brigade followed the Snake River—right through Twin Falls—to trade with the Shoshone tribe at Bear Lake (near Montpelier, Idaho).

By 1824 the Americans were back in the fur business but in the Rocky Mountains. After dogging Ross's brigade to the Salmon River, Jedediah Smith's party explored eastward up the Snake River. Joseph Walker, Capt. Benjamin Bonneville, and others who found the Northwest Company's Shoshone brigade trail along the Snake River, explored westward. The Americans were again in competition with the British, this time for the beaver of Dry and Rock Creeks (and other familiar streams in the present counties of Twin Falls, Cassia, and Owyhee).

American trappers, then called "mountain men," trapped beaver in and around the Rockies where they held annual spring trade fairs for almost twenty years. The Rendezvous made the traditional trading posts obsolete. The fur company's caravans arrived at the Rendezvous with a hundred mules packed high with supplies and trade goods, and after a few weeks of revelry, they returned to St. Louis loaded with furs.

In this way the American fur traders established a route from St. Louis along the Platte River and beyond the mountains to Bear Lake, just as the British had established a route from their trade center on the Columbia along the Snake River to that same lake. The two trade routes joined to form the Overland Trail on which men and horses and mules crossed the continent for two more decades, traveling through Twin Falls.

The Overland Trail Became the Oregon Trail

Before the beaver was all trapped out in the 1840s, certain mountain men took their own wagons along this overland route one leg at a time. The first leg was covered in 1830 when Bill Sublette took nine mule-drawn wagons in his fur company's trade caravan to Rendezvous just to prove it could be done. Missionaries began to go to Oregon in the 1830s. They traveled with the American caravan as far as Rendezvous and the rest of the way with the British brigade. A few missionaries took their own wagons, but when they reached Fort Hall, which was then owned by the Hudson's Bay Fur Company, the British insisted that they leave their wagons there and go the rest of the way by pack animal.

One missionary, Dr. Marcus Whitman, was determined to take his party's two wagons all the way. The first wagon broke down at Fort Laramie. At Fort Hall the second one gave out and Whitman reduced it to a cart, which he got as far as Fort Boise. These were the first wheels to go through Twin Falls. In Dr. Whitman's party were his wife Narcissa and the Spaldings, Henry and Eliza. The two missionary wives were the first white women to go overland to Oregon—and right through Twin Falls. The year was 1836.

In 1840 an out-of-work trapper Robert "Doc" Newell guided a small party of missionaries from the last Rendezvous to Fort Hall. The missionaries gave their wagons to Doc in payment for his services and took pack animals from there as instructed by the British. Newell knew that the British could prevent American settlement of Oregon by "appropriating" wagons, especially those of homesteaders. He sent for his mountain-man friend and brother-in-law Joe Meek (they had married Indian sisters), and Joe arrived with their families and four more out-of-work trappers. This party took those three wagons on the last leg of the Overland Trail to Dr. Whitman's mission near the Columbia River.

> *The Doctor shook me heartily by the hand. Mrs. Whitman, too, welcomed us, and the Indians walked around our wagons, or what they called "horse canoes," and seemed to give up.* —Robert Newell, 1840

So the wagon road that was blazed along the fur traders' Overland Trail by these mountain men was proof that wagons could get across the country to the rich farmland of Oregon. That's all the homesteaders were waiting for. In the Great Migration of 1843, almost one thousand pioneers, guided by none other than Dr. Marcus Whitman, were the first to take their wagons all the way to Oregon. On their new wagon road, which they dubbed the "Oregon Trail," emigrants went through Twin Falls as fast as they could.

It is nothing else than a wild, rocky barren wilderness of wrecked and ruined Nature, a vast field of volcanic desolation.

—O. Johnson and W. H. Winter, 1843 emigrants

At a camp on the Snake River at "The Cedars" (Milner Dam location) the travelers could see the Snake River begin its drop into a deep canyon and its rushing waters become inaccessible. From that camp their captains headed the wagon trains southwest in search of creeks out of the South Hills for campsites. Two days later they made camp on Rock Creek. Along Rock Creek were Indian fishing camps as well as the cold campsites of Wilson P. Hunt's 1811 party and Robert Stuart's Astorians returning east in 1812.

We ascended the bluffs early, and following the trace in 9 miles S.E. crossed precipice creek [Rock Creek], *up which we continued 14 more and encamped.* —Robert Stuart, 28 August 1812

While sporadically accompanying the Great Migration in 1843, Lt. John C. Fremont made the first map of the area showing the name "Rock Creek" where his second expedition encamped, as did the emigrants.

A melancholy and strange country—one of fracture and violence, and fire. —Lt. John C. Fremont, 1843 expedition

Water hard to reach. Poor country, soil is sandy loam and mucky clay, which when dry flies like lime. Only sage brush will grow here.

—James Clyman, ex–mountain man and 1844 emigrant

No time was lost in traveling over this "barren wilderness" on their Oregon Trail, the only road through Twin Falls for the next twenty years.

The Oregon Trail Became the Overland Stage Road

Gold was discovered in the remote Boise Basin in 1862, and the basin was flooded with thousands of miners who demanded mail and freight service. Freight came from Salt Lake City by pack-animal trains on narrow trails because there were no freight roads until 1864. That year the first permanent establishment was constructed in Twin Falls by Ben Holladay, the "Stagecoach King." Holladay had a government contract to carry the mail between Salt Lake City and Walla Walla in Washington Territory by way of Fort Boise. To establish his first Overland Mail and Stage Road, Holladay fixed up the abandoned Fort Hall and built relay stations ten to fifteen miles apart on the well-worn Oregon Trail. He chose the watering hole at Rock Creek, midway to Fort Boise, for a home station to provide meals for stagecoach passengers and lodging for attendants and off-duty drivers.

Conflicts arose between Bannock Indians and stagecoach employees at the relay stations. To protect the mail the commander at Fort Boise set up Camp Reed at Rock Creek, then moved it to near Salmon Falls (above Hagerman), and soldiers escorted the Overland Stage through hostile Indian country during the fall of 1865. That year James Bascom and John Corder built a log store next to Holladay's Rock Creek Stage Station and had the only trading post on the Oregon Trail and Overland Stage Road between Fort Hall and Fort Boise.

Holladay sold his stage line to Wells Fargo in 1866. The business saw other changes of owners and mail contracts by 1869 when the transcontinental railroad was completed. Thirty-five miles west of Promontory in Utah Territory, where the gold spike was driven to join the Union Pacific and Central Pacific Railroads, was the Kelton terminal. From Kelton, John Hailey opened a new mail and stage route into Idaho Territory by way of the City of Rocks, Oakley, and Dry Creek to join the Overland Stage Road at Rock Creek Station. This became known as the Kelton Road. Partners Arthur D. Norton and Milo G. Robinson used this Kelton Road for running their freight wagons from Ogden, Utah.

Gold Was Discovered in the Snake River

No sooner were the two railroads joined than the news was spread that gold was discovered in the Snake River Canyon. Miners came from the Boise Basin and elsewhere to work claims from Hagerman to Cauldron Linn covering a distance of sixty river miles. Two mining camps sprang up just eight miles north and east of the Rock Creek Station: a camp called Shoshone below the Twin Falls and one called Drytown at the mouth of Dry Creek (below Murtaugh).

With the completion of the transcontinental railroad, the many Chinese who had labored on the Central Pacific were left jobless in Corinne, Utah. When they heard of gold in the Snake River, many headed north on the new Kelton Road, stopping at Rock Creek Station on their way to the camps. The Snake River miners held a convention in May 1870 and agreed to prevent more Chinese from entering the area—by means of escort and threats. Drytown was panned out by August, and that autumn the ban on Chinese emigration was repealed. The gold played out at Shoshone camp the next year. When that camp was abandoned, the first post office in Twin Falls was moved from Shoshone camp to Bascom's store at Rock Creek Station.

The largest camp, Springtown, grew up between the other two camps and was deep in the canyon. The south side was reached by a narrow, winding trail down to the "town in shadow;" the north side by precarious wooden ladders that descended the north wall. In 1875 a nineteen-year-old man from Iowa, Charlie Walgamott, stopped at the Rock Creek Station, which was managed by his brother-in-law Charles and sister Irene Trotter; then he ventured on to Springtown to do some placer mining. In Springtown he found:

> *. . . several general stores, the largest run by Herman Stricker and John Botzet, four saloons, a dance hall, and a ferry.*
>
> —Charlie Walgamott, 1875

When gold played out and miners left the camps, many of them transferred their claims to Chinese miners. In some cases, where Chinese men had worked for other miners for wages, claims were turned over to them in lieu of paying them in precious gold dust. Springtown was the last Snake

River gold camp to be abandoned. In 1879 Springtown was described by an English traveler as "a hamlet composed of a few miserable Chinese huts."

Historical Update: *Along one area near Springtown, Chinese miners built small, terraced gardens and raised herbs and vegetables. The remains of several Chinese shelters are still present in the canyon* [below Hansen Bridge]. —Ron James, Twin Falls historian (1995)

Rock Creek Station Grew into a Settlement

Following the Union Pacific Railroad construction westward, Civil War veteran Herman Stricker and his partner John Botzet supplied food at the construction camps from a commissary wagon. At Promontory in 1869 they heard of the gold strike on the Snake River and took their commissary wagon up the Kelton Road to the gold camps. At Springtown they built a store. In 1876 with the gold and the miners almost gone from the river, the partners bought Bascom's store and post office at Rock Creek Station.

The stage arrived at Rock Creek about 8 o'clock where an excellent breakfast was awaiting the hungry wayfarers. Mr. Charles Trotter keeps the house here, and he and his estimable wife spare no pains in their effort to make this a desirable resting place.

—W. A. Goulder, travel correspondent, 21 July 1876

The busy stage station store continued to prosper. Customers included stagecoach passengers and drivers, emigrants in covered wagons, freight line mule skinners, Indians, ranchers and cowboys from the new cattle ranches in the area, and an occasional "bad man." Chinese miners had a "China house" near the station for their recreation. "Rock Creek" became a community with a dance hall and a school.

Three years after the store changed hands, Charlie Walgamott's sister Lucy came to Rock Creek Station to visit their sister, Mr. Charles Trotter's "estimable wife" Irene. There Lucy met Herman Stricker, and in 1882 she and Herman were married.

> *When her organ arrived at the Rock Creek Station, Lucy gave the cowboys and travelers a concert.*
>
> —Gladys Stricker, one of Lucy and Herman's seven children (1960)

> *Got to Rock Creek. The station of Rock Creek is a town of 8 or 10 buildings situated on Rock Creek. . . . An outfit of 8 or 10 wagons came into town soon after we did.*
>
> —Will M. Brabb, emigrant to Oregon from Missouri, 28 July 1882

All that good commerce was about to be disrupted. In 1883 the Oregon Short Line Railroad from Minidoka reached Shoshone, a settlement thirty-three miles north of Rock Creek. Expecting a boom in tourism, Herman Stricker's new brother-in-law Charlie Walgamott moved to Shoshone and went into the tourist business. Charlie and his partner hewed out a road from the north canyon rim to Shoshone Falls where they set up a tent hotel. Then they ran daily coach trips to their resort establishing the Shoshone Road. Next they built a ferry across the Snake River above the falls, making possible a connection with the freight road that Norton and Robinson had established on the south side between Rock Creek and the gold camps. Here was a convenient new route where mail, passengers, and freight could come to Rock Creek Station from nearby Shoshone rather than the distant Kelton. The Kelton Road and the Overland Stage Lines were no longer necessary. The stage station at Rock Creek became obsolete, and the Stricker-Botzet store lost its business.

With the prospect of another store going out of business, Herman Stricker completed a ditch that was started for irrigation and put to work the appropriation of 500 inches of Rock Creek water he and John Botzet filed on; John deeded his interests to Herman. Stricker went to work on his 960 acres of farm and would continue to operate his store and post office another fourteen years in the dwindling community of Rock Creek.

A Second Rock Creek Settlement Filled the Void

Three men were sitting on their horses having a visit, and they decided they needed another store.

—Don Dean, president, Twin Falls County Historical Society, 1998

One of the three men, Joseph F. Tatro, built a store two miles upstream from Rock Creek. In spite of the failure of Rock Creek's businesses after the railroad reached Shoshone, Tatro's little store started a new settlement in the developing cattle country. Here ranching was called "farming" because of the need to irrigate with water from Rock Creek to grow winter feed for the livestock.

The first cattle—four hundred head of Texas longhorns—were brought by way of Cheyenne in 1871 by Arthur Norton and Milo Robinson to supply the miners with beef. These were the partners who also ran a freight line to the Snake River gold camps; in Drytown they had a store. Their cattle ranch was on Cottonwood Creek four miles west of Rock Creek Station. They wintered their herds where the Twin Falls townsite would later be founded. The decline in gold mining forced Robinson to sell his interest to Norton, and in the 1880s the 71 brand of the Norton Cattle Company ranged west to Three Creek.

A. J. Harrell from California had a herd of from three to four thousand head of Texas longhorns wintering in Nevada. In the spring of 1872 he drove them up to the Goose Creek Mountains (south of Burley) for summer range. Under this routine the herd increased to twenty-four thousand head. One of his Idaho ranches (the Brose home) was on Rock Creek a mile south of Rock Creek Station. Harrell's was the Shoesole brand.

John Sparks from Texas bought out two small Rock Creek ranches; John Tinnan of Wyoming bought the Winecup and HD brands of Nevada. In 1882 they became partners in the Sparks-Tinnan Company and bought Harrell's Shoesole with its herd of 175,000 head. By then Shoesole cattle ranged from Oakley to the Bruneau River and from the Snake River to the Great American Desert in Nevada to become the second largest cattle outfit in the United States.

Sparks had a contract with the government to haul the mail. When the Central Pacific Railroad built the Lucin Cutoff across the Great Salt Lake bypassing Kelton, Montello in Nevada became the new terminal. From that point Sparks's stages took a circuitous route with stops at his six ranches before continuing north over the South Hills with mail and passengers bound for Rock Creek. (Sparks's Overland Stage Road is now called the Rock Creek Canyon Road.) Tatro built his store on Sparks's Overland Stage Road.

When Milo Robinson bought Tatro's store, next door was Domrose's hotel, and across the street was L. Pete Larsen's candy and cigar store and a pool hall. This growing community was usually called "Upper Rock Creek" because the dwindling settlement downstream at Stricker's store was still being referred to as Rock Creek. Herman Stricker closed his store in 1897, transferred the post office to a store in Upper Rock Creek in 1899, and continued to farm and ranch. In 1900 John F. Hansen of Albion bought the Tatro store in Upper Rock Creek.

John Hansen and his brother Lawrence, both born in Denmark, arrived in Cassia County from Indiana in 1876 and found work on a ranch at Cottonwood twenty miles east of Rock Creek. John worked there only that summer and taught school that winter. The next year the brothers came to the Rock Creek area. While John worked for Herman Stricker at his store, Lawrence established a ranch a few miles upstream from the Rock Creek Station. Lawrence would become a prominent stockman, a member of the Idaho legislature, and chairman of the Board of Trustees of Albion State Normal School when established in 1893. Lawrence's wife Mary, his two daughters, and John's bride Anna Petersen arrived from Indiana that year, 1877.

> *What he* [Lawrence Hansen] *did not know was that the southern part of his homestead was used every year as a winter camp for a considerable number of Indians who spent their summers in the Shoshone Basin, a unit of the Goose Creek Mountain range. . . . The older Indians explained they had come somewhat earlier this year because they wanted to be on time for the first run of salmon. They were as much surprised to see a house nearby as the Hansens were to see wigwams.*
>
> —Anna Hansen Hayes, niece of Lawrence Hansen (1963)

John and Anna were married on 2 September 1877—the first wedding in Twin Falls. They moved back to Cottonwood to start a cheese factory, and there baby Anna (the future Mrs. John E. Hayes) and Carrie (the future

Mrs. George Crockett) were born. John met the Cassia County surveyor Frank Riblett whose 1881 irrigation plan for the Snake River got John's support. John was named Cassia County superintendent of schools in 1892, and the Hansens moved to Albion, the county seat. There John met I. B. Perrine who marketed his produce in that town. In 1900 Hansen moved his family, then with six children, to Upper Rock Creek and purchased the Tatro store where he would sell Perrine's produce.

The new settlement grew with a school and a meat market, a bowling alley, community hall, dance hall, two public corrals, five saloons, and a "honky-tonk," the Wooden Shoe.

> *Remember the 4th of July celebrations in Rock Creek when everyone from Oakley to Three Creeks came for the entire day? We had foot races, horse races, games, jumping contests for all ages, and a whopping big picnic. Why, we kids looked forward to that day from one year to the next. All that fun and excitement didn't cost our folks a cent. . . . There were dances in the public hall until sunrise with Lucy Stricker at the organ. . . . On New Year's Eve there were masquerades and on Washington's Birthday character balls were held.*
>
> —Charlotte W. Crockett, daughter-in-law of Carrie Hansen Crockett (1963)

But Upper Rock Creek's days were numbered. A population of forty-four was recorded in the 1880 census of the Rock Creek area. In that decade the ranchers were able to purchase the first water rights to Rock Creek. They saw success until overgrazing, the droughts from 1886 to 1890, and the terrible winters with frozen, rain-crusted snow caused the cattle industry as a whole to suffer a 65 percent loss. Ranchers sold out and left. In 1891 A. J. Harrell and his son Andrew bought out Tinnan's interest in Sparks-Tinnan, and the business became Sparks-Harrell Company. John Sparks sold out to the Harrells and left for Virginia City, Nevada, to become governor of that state. When the Harrells sold out to the Vineyard Land and Stock Company of Ogden, Utah, that outfit then owned the Shoesole. The 1900 census showed a population in the Rock Creek community of only 146.

The range was a loss; it never recovered. Between 1890 and 1900, with cattle numbers greatly reduced and the territory opening up and getting settled, more sheep were trailed in from Oregon and California. Idaho had three million sheep free-grazing on public land—"range sheep of the West"—that ranged from Glenns Ferry to American Falls and wintered in the Nevada desert. When this system was ended by coyotes, a ban on poison, fees and flock reductions by the government, sheepmen reverted to "farm flocks."

> *Sheepmen had great respect for each other even though they were highly competitive in their business. Buying and selling was done with a handshake, their philosophy: If you can't trust a man's word, what's the use of having his name on a piece of paper?*
>
> —Miriam B. Breckenridge, sheep rancher (1963)

Historical Update: One man who trailed sheep from Oregon to Idaho was a Nebraskan, the great grandfather of State Senator Laird Noh who has represented Twin Falls for the past twenty-three years. When Noh retires, his son John will take over the family ranch in Twin Falls County to be the fifth generation in the local sheep business.

The Stricker log residence burned down, and a Victorian farmhouse (extant today) was constructed in 1900 with three bedrooms downstairs and several rooms upstairs. When the Twin Falls Irrigation Project began in 1903, Lucy Stricker—with six children then—turned her house into a sort of hotel for men working on the canal system.

> *Before the Twin Falls Tract was open, dances were held at the Shoesole Ranch, the Brose home, and the Stricker home where there was room for two squares of dancers accompanied by Lucy playing the organ. . . . At her home Lucy entertained homesick canal workers, gave them a dinner and dance and breakfast.*
>
> —Gladys Stricker

The Utah Cattle Company of Ogden, which bought out several small ranches in southcentral Idaho, became the Utah Construction Company (UCC) and obtained contracts to build canals and the railroad using fresnos, slip scrapers, plows, men with shovels, and horses and mules supplied with hay from its local ranches. By 1905 the canal system and railroad stretched from Burley to Buhl and thousands of acres were cleared of sagebrush, plowed, planted, and irrigated for homesteads.

> [Frank Hobbs] *told me one day he was after a bunch of* [Shoesole] *cattle down on the Twin Falls Tract and started to ride across a patch of plowed ground. An old farmer came out after him with a rifle. Frank said, "You old son of a gun, if you think you are going to use that on me, I'll rope you and drag you to death right here."* As Frank *started unbuckling his riata, the farmer dropped his gun and started for the house. . . . We had quite a lot of trouble with the farmers in one way or another, but most of them were nice folks.*
>
> —Thomas Ike Gray, cowboy (1988)

The irrigation system changed what was left of the rangeland, and the once wonderful southern Idaho grazing country was finally lost to the ranchers who could no longer turn their cattle loose. With construction of the canals came the settlement of the town of Twin Falls.

> *To make an all day trip to town, one hung a white dish towel on the clothes line so the other, down the road, could see it and have time to get her eggs and cream and herself ready to go. The trip took all day by wagon or buggy.* —Pearl M. Rayl, homesteader

When the railroad reached the settlement of Twin Falls in 1905, the smaller stage lines with government mail contracts all but ceased operation in the area. The post office was again located at Strickers'—in their farmhouse—from 1905 to 1910, then it moved back to Upper Rock Creek. In 1908 Vineyard sold the Shoesole to UCC, which had helped bring the railroad to Twin Falls—then came the automobile. After rural mail delivery began in 1912, many community post offices closed including Upper Rock Creek's. Its store closed in 1916, and Upper Rock Creek faded away like so many hopeful little farm and ranch towns in southcentral Idaho.

Historical Update: All that remains of Upper Rock Creek is a dilapidated little post office. Not far away, at the Historic Stricker Homesite, the Old Farmhouse watches from its front porch as the combined Oregon Trail, Overland Mail and Stage Road, and Kelton Road pass by on their way to the Historic Rock Creek Stage Station. All that remains today of that 1864 station with its barn for twelve horses and a blacksmith shop is a rock outline of the foundation. Only the Rock Creek Store—the oldest building in Twin Falls and Cassia Counties and known locally as the "Stricker Store"—remains to testify to pre–Twin Falls History between 1865 and 1904.

STRICKER STORE

Suggested Reading Available at the Twin Falls Public Library

From the Astorians to the Oregon Trail

- *On the Oregon Trail*, Robert Stuart's Journal of Discovery 1812–1813
- *Ogden's Snake Country Journals 1827–1829*: The Hudson's Bay Record Society 1971
- *Across the Wide Missouri*, Bernard DeVoto, 1947
- *Land of Giants*, David Lavender, 1956
- *Astoria*, Washington Irving, 1836
- *Oregon Trail*, Ingvard Eide, 1972
- *Fort Hall, Gateway to Oregon Country*, Frank Robertson, 1936
- *Bill Sublette*, John E. Sunder, 1959
- *No Man Like Joe*, Harvey Tobie, 1949
- *A Majority of Scoundrels*, Don Berry, 1961
- *The Traveler's Guide to the Oregon Trail*, Julie Fanselow,* 1992

From Rock Creek Station to Ranching

- *Idaho of Yesterday*, Thomas Donaldson, 1941
- *The Wake of the Prairie Schooner*, Irene Paden, 1943
- *Stagecoach West*, Ralph Moody, 1967
- *Only the Mountains Remain*, Nora Bowman, 1958

- *Six Decades Back*, Charles Walgamott,* 1936
- *A Brief Summary: John E. Hayes*, Anna Hayes,* 1967
- *Buckskin and Smoke*, Anna Hayes,* 1971
- *Ruins of a World*, Ron James,* 1995
- *Scattered Graves*, Kestler, Meyers, & Holloway,* 1998
- *Zest for Living*, Lorayne Smith,* 1991
- *Life in the Saddle*, Karen Quinton,* 1988
- *Territorial Centennial Twin Falls County 1863–1963*
- *Idaho State Centennial: Local History 1890–1990*

* Local Magic Valley authors

Chapter 2

The Irrigation Project

The greatest irrigation project in the U.S.A., and the third largest in the world. —Irrigation Age, December 1903, Vol. XIX, No. 2 Chicago

Ira Burton Perrine, A.K.A. I. B. or Bert—Never Ira

He is a little fellow . . . and he's always the same genial, thoughtful, enthusiastic, optimistic, gentleman. With him I met hundreds of men and every one of them was as glad to see "Bert" as though he were their partner. —C. E. Churchill, advertiser, New York 1918

In 1883 when the Oregon Short Line Railroad reached Shoshone in Idaho Territory, Bert Perrine, twenty-two years old and fresh out of college, boarded that train in Pocatello. He rode to Shoshone where he had an aunt and an uncle, B. W. Burton. From Shoshone Bert took the stage to Bullion, a booming mining camp near Hailey, where he found work in a mine. Before long he was robbed of the first hundred dollars he saved, which he carried on his person. He decided he was too small for the rough mines, and Bert Perrine, who grew up on a farm in Indiana, switched to the dairy business to supply the miners with milk. To find pasture for his herd Bert drove his twenty-five cows from Hailey to Shoshone, a distance of forty-five miles.

In the fall of 1884, Bert drove his cows another twenty-five miles to Shoshone Falls to consult with Charlie Walgamott. Charlie took Bert and his herd

three miles down along the Snake River to a deep, broad valley in the canyon that had plenty of pasture and two very blue lakes that never froze. This was just what Bert needed for wintering his small dairy herd, and he filed a claim on the valley naming it "Blue Lakes."

Charlie also took Bert Perrine to the Rock Creek area where, in the 1880s, ranchers could purchase water rights to Rock Creek. When Bert saw the hay, grain, vegetables, and fruit produced by those settlers through irrigation, he recognized the larger potential of his little pasture. With water from a ditch of an abandoned placer mine, Bert started his canyonland ranch by planting fruit trees. (Over time, I. B. Perrine would add grapes, melons, berries, then sheep to establish his thousand-acre Blue Lakes Ranch and Fruit Company.)

To finance his new venture Bert sold his herd, and with a partner, a miner named Tom Hyndman, purchased a livery stable in Shoshone, got a coach and some horses, and ran a stage line to Shoshone Falls. Their posters read:

EXCURSION TO SHOSHONE FALLS
June 26, 1886

> *The new* [Dewey] *hotel is open to guests. Now is your opportunity to visit the great "Niagara of the West" as special rates will be given on this occasion. The stage will leave on this Saturday evening and return Sunday evening. For particulars see Bert Perrine at Shoshone Livery Stable.*
> —The Perrine Family Archives

An Indian trail, which was Bert's only access to his Blue Lakes ranch, could not accommodate his stagecoach, so he took a pickax and shovel and hewed out a wagon road on the north wall of the canyon. This he completed in 1891. The next year, Bert married Hortense McKay whose father owned the Lincoln Hotel in Shoshone. Then Bert built what people would call a "hotel" at Blue Lakes.

> *The Perrines called it a boardinghouse—even a prominent guest* [Jay Gould Jr, son of the railroad magnate] *slept on the floor. Guests usually stayed at the main house.*
> —Phyllis Perrine, daughter-in-law of Ledyard, I. B.'s youngest brother, (2000)

The partners opened a road from Shoshone to Blue Lakes, called it appropriately "Blue Lakes Road," and ran a daily stage to the Blue Lakes hotel. They also continued their scenic tours to Shoshone Falls. In 1895 Bert bought out Tom's interest, his brother Silas joined him, and the Perrine brothers continued to run the stage line to support the expanding fruit business.

But Bert was handicapped for markets. All he had was a wagon run to the Wood River mines and a storefront in Shoshone. His trip to the new Albion State Normal School with a wagonload of strawberries was tortuous: out of the canyon at Blue Lakes, into and out of the canyon at Walgamott's ferry at Shoshone Falls, all before proceeding to Albion. So Bert built his own ferry across the Snake River at Blue Lakes in 1896 and started to hand-hew a wagon road on the south face of the canyon. After switching to blasting powder, Perrine completed that road—which ran behind the falls of the coulee that would bear his name—in 1898.

With a ferry and the very steep south wall road—and with extra horses available to help with the climb—Bert got a contract to carry mail between Shoshone and Rock Creek. Usually the stage went via Blue Lakes where the few remaining placer miners picked up their mail. But when carrying passengers, the stage went by way of Shoshone Falls since the Shoshone Road was the more popular route with tourists. And finally, the Perrine brothers extended their Shoshone-Rock Creek Stage Line to Oakley and Albion where Bert had established more markets for his fruit.

While Bert Perrine busily established his Blue Lakes Ranch and markets, his relatives and many friends in the area told him stories like the following. Idaho became a U.S. Territory in 1863 after the discovery of gold in the Boise Basin and the arrival of thousands of miners. A dozen years later when its gold was all but gone, the Territory was considered a "good-for-nothing desert" and Idaho was about to be partitioned among Wyoming Territory and the states of Oregon and Montana. To preserve his Territory's integrity, Gov. John B. Neil urged his seventeen counties to report their developable resources. Frank Riblett, engineer for the newly created Cassia County, made a general southcentral Idaho survey in 1879. In 1881 Riblett presented his plans for a partial dam (where Minidoka Dam is today) and gravity canals to divert water from the Snake River to the rich volcanic soils on both sides of the river. The enormous potential value of this "dirt gold" saved Idaho Territory from partition. The speech made in Congress by Idaho's territorial delegate Fred T. Dubois contributed not only to the creation of the state of Idaho in 1890 but also to the eventual development of the Snake River Plain.

In 1894 Congress passed the Carey Act written by Sen. Joseph M. Carey of Wyoming. Under the Carey Act the federal government could donate one million acres of arid land to each state that would construct canals and have the land reclaimed within ten years. The following year, Idaho Gov. William J. McConnell accepted the gift and the legislature passed Idaho's first district irrigation law.

> *It was in 1895 that we first knew Mr. Perrine when he came to Albion on a fruit-selling trip. . . . From time to time, as he came to sell his harvest, he stopped at our house for a visit, sometimes for a meal or to stay overnight. During those visits, he talked with my father* [John F. Hansen] *and Frank Riblett about the plans these two had made for irrigation of what we know as the Magic Valley.*
>
> —Anna Hansen Hayes

Riblett's friend and promoter John F. Hansen had done a survey at The Cedars (where Milner Dam is today) for a health-seeking capitalist living in the area who lost his chance for developing his water diversion plan in the panic of 1890, and his health failed. Clearly, Riblett's and Hansen's exciting stories, added to the timeliness of the Carey Act and Idaho's participation in it, set Bert's imagination reeling with the possibilities of irrigation-farming in arid southcentral Idaho using Snake River water.

Irrigation of the Snake River Plain Was Not a Slam Dunk

Before Perrine's irrigation plans got moving, a roadblock was set up. Those sight-seeing excursions that both Walgamott and the Perrines made to Shoshone Falls accommodated some pretty important men who took reports of superb scenery back to Washington, D.C. In 1898 the U.S. Park Commission prepared to send inspectors to view the Middle Snake River with the object of creating a national park preserve, which would put the river's water off limits to any irrigation project. The federal land to be studied, on both sides of the Snake River from The Cedars to the Blue Lakes, was put on hold.

Nevertheless, in June 1900 a confident I. B. Perrine filed with the state of Idaho for 3,000 cubic feet per second of Snake River water. The next month he filed for 270,000 acres of land on both sides of the river at The Cedars. In August the State Land Board ordered a survey of the proposed acreage. That survey, made by State Engineer D. W. Ross assisted by J. H. Lowell, Bert Perrine, and Bert's uncle B. W. Burton, proved the feasibility of irrigating the acreage. In October, Ross granted Perrine water rights for 3,400 cubic feet per second on both sides of The Cedars.

Meanwhile, Perrine incorporated the working company required by the state and named it the Twin Falls Land and Water Company (TFL&WC). The investors he found to manage the company were Stanley B. Milner, president and general manager; I. B. Perrine, vice president; J. H. Lowell, secretary; Frank Knox, treasurer; and Albert K. (A. K.) Steunenberg, member of the board. Secretary Lowell put in a request for a segregation of 248,667 acres—which were still tied up in the national park preserve study. This team was very confident, and with good reason. During the time that Perrine made applications for water and land and organized his company, Congress had to be convinced that agricultural uses of the Snake River would serve southcentral Idaho better than a national park preserve. Gov. Frank Steunenberg appointed Frank Gooding and J. H. Lowell to go to Washington and do the lobbying. Gooding was an influential sheepman (and future Idaho governor), and Lowell was not only secretary of the TFL&WC but also head of the Boise Land and Water Company. The success of these lobbyists was never in doubt. On 1 July 1901 the on-hold land was released in favor of irrigation. Perrine had all the right connections.

A new survey had to be done to satisfy the "feds" that there was an ample supply of water for the irrigation project. This was accomplished by October by U.S. Chief Engineer A. J. Wiley assisted by Walter G. Filer—an engineer sent by Milner because he didn't trust the government. Finally, the Twin Falls Land and Water Company had its water and its land and could proceed with the project. Nothing would come easily, and it would not come at all except for the prodigious imagination and energy, optimism and enthusiasm, vision and persuasiveness of one Ira Burton Perrine, then forty years old.

Perrine's Investors Were Outstanding Men

Where or how Perrine found some of his investors is not clear. When Bert filed on his Blue Lakes land, he considered placer mining at its lower end. In 1890 Stanley B. Milner moved his family from Wisconsin to Salt Lake City, Utah, and formed the Milner Corporation, a mining investment company. Bert met Milner, interested him in his Snake River gold possibilities, and they entered into a partnership. When in 1900 Bert presented his irrigation plans, Milner invested in his proposal even though irrigation was outside this miner's milieu. It seems no one could resist Bert Perrine. With the largest investment, Milner was named president of the Twin Falls Land and Water Company.

Board member A. K. Steunenberg was a Caldwell banker whose brother was Gov. Frank Steunenberg. A. K. and secretary J. H. Lowell from Roswell favored turning the irrigation project over to the state for construction. But treasurer Frank Knox, a Salt Lake City banker associate of Milner's with only ten shares in the TFL&WC, swung the vote in favor of Milner and Perrine's intention to build with private capital. Steunenberg and Lowell left the company.

Without these two key investors, the TFL&WC was in need of new capital. Once again it would come from back east, from mining and engineering interests with no expertise in irrigation. Working with Stanley B. Milner was a civil engineer named Walter G. Filer from Sharon, Pennsylvania, whose friend Frank Buhl was a millionaire investor in the Sharon Iron Mills. Filer arranged for Buhl and his wife to come in November 1902 for a tour of the proposed irrigation project area, and Perrine won them over too. Buhl had a business associate in Sharon—with a corporate office in Chicago—named Peter Kimberly who also became an investor.

Congress passed a Reclamation Act in 1902 giving the federal government the means to advance money to states to implement the Carey Act. Private companies could then contract for the work to be done on the irrigation projects. Frank Buhl and Peter Kimberly formed the Buhl-Kimberly Corporation and contracted with the state of Idaho to build Milner Dam.

Along with this Reclamation Act a new federal department was created, the U.S. Reclamation Service (renamed the Bureau of Reclamation in 1923), which began its survey of the Milner Dam site in December. Not one to overlook any vital details, Perrine claimed the waters of Jackson Lake in

Wyoming figuring they were necessary to his project. The Reclamation Service decided to build the dam there itself (done in 1907) rather than to allow private capital to do the job.

With the infusion of eastern capital the Twin Falls Land and Water Company was re-incorporated on 14 January 1903 to contract for the Twin Falls Southside Tract (Canal) Project. Frank Buhl, who made the largest investment, was named president; Stanley B. Milner became vice president. General Manager Walter G. Filer had brought in two more mining associates that became investors: Mark Murtaugh was named his assistant manager and Paul Bickel became the chief engineer. Martin DeLong, a relative of Buhl's, invested in the company and was named secretary-treasurer. DeLong's homestead at Milner was used as company headquarters until the Northside Canal Company built the Milner Hotel.

The Work Got Underway

The first bridge spanned the Snake River at Milner in February 1903, and construction on Milner Dam began the next month.

> *. . . construction camps exceed 30 in number . . . about 400 teams and 500 men are engaged on the canal and dam . . . water is hoisted to the rim and hauled some 5–6 miles.*
>
> —*The Chicago Record-Herald*, 19 December 1903

MILNER DAM 1903

The new Twin Falls Land and Water Company issued 240,000 shares at one dollar per share. The rights to their 276,000 acre-feet of water sold at twenty-five dollars per acre-foot. Water was to be delivered to within one-half mile of each 160-acre tract, which was all one person was allowed under the Carey Act. Land was sold at fifty cents an acre with twenty-five cents per acre down and the remainder to be paid after final proof was made. The cost of hiring someone to prepare land for irrigation, including removal of sagebrush, grading, harrowing, and planting, could be between three and five dollars per acre, up to ten times the cost of the land.

Land sales, which were held in Shoshone in July, were slow because of little publicity and promotion by the TFL&WC. Of only fifty-seven prospective homesteaders there, just thirty filed for Carey Act land. Something had to be done, and just one man could do it.

I. B. Perrine incorporated his Twin Falls Investment Company in June the following year, and his company signed a contract with the TFL&WC to sell 25,000 acres a year. The company's officers were C. B. Hurtt, president; I. B. Perrine, vice president and general western manager; Thomas Costello, vice president and general eastern manager; Robert McCollum, secretary; J. Crocker, treasurer; and George F. Sprague, assistant treasurer. With Bob McCollum's promotional skills and Tom Costello's eastern connections, all the land would get sold, and not one acre would revert for lack of payment.

Establishing a homestead was not easy to do. The Carey Act required a homesteader to select his land, establish residence with a prove-up shack, clear and put crops in one-eighth of his acreage. That done, he would advertise a certain number of times in the newspaper his intentions to make final proof and appear before the land commissioner with three witnesses to swear to his compliance with the law. The commissioner would inspect the property and pass final proof. This process could take several years.

A prove-up shack in Sucker Flat—settled north of Filer by people from Illinois, the "Sucker State"—was described by a homesteader:

> *These were usually one room, box-like structures built as temporary housing until a more permanent type could be built. Most had a roof of foot-wide boards with bats over the cracks. One soon learned to sweep the snow off the roof before building a fire or else have plenty of pots and pans available. Not everything was bad in pioneer life—fuel was plentiful: sagebrush stalks for cook stove and brushy part for*

heater. Meat abundant: rabbits everywhere: shoot it, skin it, nail it on the north side of the shack for good eating and too high for dogs to get. Sage hens were everywhere and tasted like sagebrush.

—John T. Parish

PROVE-UP SHACK

And so the land was settled. Water flowed into the southside canals on 1 March 1905. The Twin Falls Land and Water Company established experimental farms offering guidance to eastern and midwestern dryfarmers, who were unfamiliar with irrigation farming, for effective use of land and water. The stockholders of the Twin Falls Southside Tract Project incorporated the Twin Falls Canal Company in 1909.

Historical Update: The irrigation project paid for itself by 1928 when all the original investors were paid in full, but the only one still living was Walter G. Filer. The Twin Falls Land and Water Company was dissolved in 1940.

Suggested Reading Available at the Twin Falls Public Library

- *Idaho's Lusty Young City*, Idaho shelf
- *How Things Happen in Twin Falls County*, League of Women Voters, 1974
- *Emigrant Trails of South Idaho*, BLM publication, 1993
- *We Sagebrush Folk*, Annie Pike Greenwood, 1991

Chapter 3

Twin Falls Townsite, 1904

The stage driven from Shoshone entered the town over Blue Lakes Blvd.—then a cleared path through the sagebrush. At the corner there was a post in the middle of the road. A sign on it stated that when the traveler had gone around the post, he was on Shoshone Street, which was just a wagon trail too. . . . There was dust a foot deep on all the main roads. Coyotes were occasionally seen chasing rabbits down Main Avenue. Even rattlesnakes were occasionally discovered on business streets.

—S. T. (Sam) Hamilton, the attorney from Colorado

The Townsite Was Prepared

The Twin Falls Land and Water Company (TFL&WC) signed a contract with the state of Idaho in January 1903 to build the canal system for the Twin Falls Southside Tract. In that contract was a provision for the establishment of townsites to support the agricultural communities that would grow with the irrigation project. For the Twin Falls townsite a school section was purchased: Sec 16, TS 10 S, R 17 E, Boise Meridian. This could be sold in lots and parcels with immediate transfer of ownership—unlike homestead land, which was subject to "proving-up" before ownership was patented, and that could take years.

The company's chief engineer Paul Bickel located the Twin Falls section and marked its corners. Bickel designated his earnest, twenty-seven-year-old assistant John E. Hayes to do the layout and surveying of the townsite. Hayes had studied under the chief engineer of the state of Colorado at age sixteen and then worked for seven years in underground mining until a serious accident in 1899. After that, Hayes worked for Paul Bickel on an examinations survey for the United States-Canadian border in Washington, Montana, and Idaho. On this Twin Falls project John Hayes would meet Anna Hansen, a daughter of John F. Hansen of Rock Creek, and they would be married on 25 December 1905. Four days later, Hayes would receive his civil engineering license to begin a long and productive career in Twin Falls.

ANNA HANSEN HAYES

Late in April 1904, Hayes and his crew started a survey of four town blocks at the center of the sage-covered section. The first plat was filed on 12 May in Albion, seat of Cassia County, under the name of Twin Falls—over the objection of many people who wanted the town named for I. B. Perrine, but he wouldn't allow it to be named for him.

> *Grandpa* [James A. Waters] *helped survey the canal system and the city of Twin Falls. They first laid the town straight with the world (north and south, east and west) but found they couldn't run water. So they laid it out diagonally and that worked out better for water. . . . They always had to watch for scorpions and dump their shoes out before putting them on.* —Jean Duffek-Nutsch, Jerome (2000)

> [The townsite was set on the diagonal] *so that every lot in the city can be irrigated by surface irrigation. The slope of the land was such that irrigation water would drain away naturally along the edges of the streets. . . . It would permit sunshine in every room.*
>
> —John E. Hayes

> *Bickel's one regret was the fierce opposition of others of that era to the wide streets he wished . . . he was forced to lay streets considerably narrow . . . he still managed to get them twice as wide as they would otherwise have been.* —The Perrine Family Archives

In June the TFL&WC incorporated a subsidiary, the Twin Falls Townsite Company, to administer the townsite until the town could have its own government. The Townsite Company contracted with I. B. Perrine's Investment Company to sell its lots and parcels and to build a luxury hotel to promote land sales "in this sagebrush country with its jackrabbits, coyotes, rattlesnakes, and scorpions; where the roads were thick with dust that the winds blew everywhere and the rains turned into mire; where there was not a spot of shade or greenery, and the sun shone relentlessly." Once the first-class hotel was built, the challenge to lure investors, settlers, and homesteaders to come and experience this "uncivilized, but promising," tract would fall to Perrine's eastern connections.

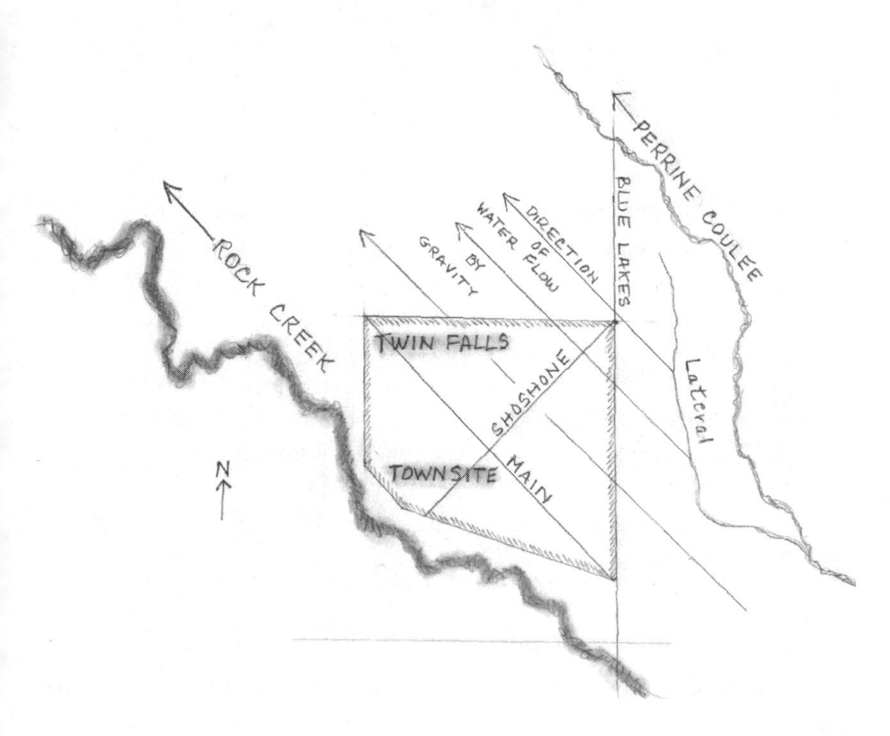

For his Investment Company's office Perrine erected the townsite's first structure, a temporary wooden shack on Main Avenue and Fourth Street S (Bill's Automotive location), and opened it for business on 27 July. The first land sale was made on 1 August to George C. Walters, an engineer on the Oregon Short Line Railroad. The Investment Company's secretary, Robert

McCollum, became such an eager land salesman, they called him "Cyclone Bob." George Sprague set up an office to sell insurance on commercial and residential properties in a tent behind Perrine's shack. As the Investment Company's assistant treasurer, Sprague was in charge of construction of the luxury hotel, and these first businesses would move their offices into his hotel for its December 1905 opening.

Survey of the townsite and the sale of its lots and parcels continued through the summer and into the fall. After less than six months, the final plat of the entire square-mile townsite was filed in Albion on 4 October 1904, and its unpopular name of Twin Falls became official.

Historical Update: The streets and avenues were originally numbered consecutively across the townsite, streets starting at the northwest corner and avenues starting at the northeast corner. The quadrant system—with streets numbered in both directions from Shoshone Street and avenues numbered in both directions from Main Avenue—was adopted in 1906. For convenience in locating sites in these stories, the quadrant naming system is used.

If You Build It, They Will Come

Commercial interests were quick to build. The Perrine and Burton Store opened on Main Avenue at Shoshone Street S (Wells Fargo location) on 23 July beating the opening of I. B.'s shack-office by four days and claiming to be "first." The Perrine half of the business was Bert's two brothers Silas and William, and the Burton half was their cousin William L. Burton. These three men had also filed on homesteads and had stores in Kimama and Milner during dam construction.

Historical Update:

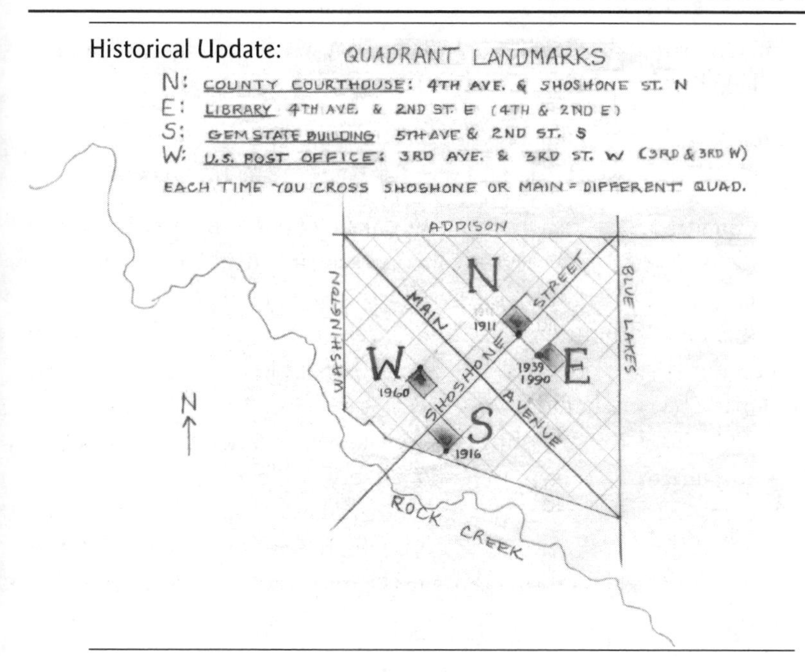

Ads in the early issues of the News *showed that the Perrine and Burton Store sold everything from shoe laces to lumber and farm machinery.*

—Phyllis Perrine

Walter Hollingsworth opened the first barber shop in a tent cabin next to the Perrine and Burton Store. He brought water from Rock Creek in tanks, dispensed it in buckets, and heated it on a stove. His haircut and massage was twenty-five cents; shave, fifteen cents; and a bath was twenty cents. Hours were 8 A.M. to 6 P.M. Monday through Friday, and 8 to 8 on Saturday; he closed Sundays. Walter's shop would have a 3-chair shoeshine parlor and a hat cleaning-and-blocking service for his well-dressed patrons coming from back east to this dusty desert. Jerry Hunt worked there for a while, then opened his own barber shop down the avenue.

In those days, tonsorial experts gave more shaves than haircuts until manufacturers began making safety razors so men could shave at home.

—Jack Hyder and Eric Goddell (1990)

Roy W. Gager opened the first hardware store behind the Perrine and Burton Store. Then he and partner M. Kennedy moved it to Main Avenue and named it Twin Falls Hardware. In 1905 they would sell their business to L. E. Salladay and Fred Wilkinson.

> *I found the Salladay name spelled Saladay and Saliday as well.*
>
> —Chris Bolton, president, Twin Falls County Historical Society, 2003

On 10 August Mrs. Prothero from Wisconsin opened the first restaurant on Second Avenue E (now the Key Bank parking lot) near George Bassett's establishment. All Mrs. Prothero's food was hauled by team from the railroad in Shoshone without refrigeration. Yet, she considered this no more an inconvenience than those "Bassett's goats" that ate her pies cooling on the bench outside her kitchen door.

George Bassett was a subcontractor for the construction of Milner Dam. In 1904 he came to Twin Falls and built a livery stable and corral on the alley at the back of his lot on Second Avenue E. That fall at the front of his lot George added his Headquarters Saloon, which was commonly known as the "Bucket of Blood." Between these two enterprises George added a dining room and a kitchen.

> *Ladies patronized the eatery but never the saloon.*
>
> —Twin Falls High School Student Publication, 1944

A fenced runway from the corral ran along the east side of his dining room, and there Bassett kept the pigs he raised for pork. They were also his garbage disposal. The rattle of knives and forks in the dining room brought the grunting pigs to the windows, and the delighted patrons threw them their leftovers; that was the dinner show.

Robert McCollum built the townsite's first permanent residence at the corner of Shoshone Street and Seventh Avenue N.

> *It was a large and ornate shanty.* —Sam Hamilton

Bob McCollum and Bert Perrine met in 1897 in Shoshone where McCollum was editor of the *Shoshone Journal*; Bob had his office in the rear of the building and Bert marketed his produce in the front. Before he filed for water rights, Bert talked Bob into being a partner in his irrigation project, then lost his support on their trip to the site of the future Milner Dam where Bob declared it "a crazy proposition." But in 1904 McCollum became involved in Perrine's Investment Company as its secretary and made the move to Twin Falls.

Robert McCollum, who was mayor, chief of police, and rabbit catcher, was the entire population of Twin Falls.

—Twin Falls High School Student Publication, 1944

The McCollum residence was at once the center of the town's social life. Mrs. McCollum noticed the many businessmen and professional men getting settled in the town before bringing their wives and families, and thinking them homesick, she invited twenty of them for dinner. So, they called themselves the "Homeless Twenty" and decided they should meet there once a week to socialize and sing songs around Alice McCollum's piano, the first in the town. Members included Paul Bickel, John E. Hayes, and Martin DeLong; S. T. Hamilton, attorney for the Twin Falls Investment Company; publisher Charles Diehl; and the town's first doctor, Henry W. Clouchek. From this group in 1905 would come Twin Falls's first civic organization, the Twin Falls Commercial Club.

Historical Update: John and Anna Hayes purchased the "ornate shanty" in 1936 and did the first remodeling. Later owners Dr. Clarence Schilt and Dr. Elwood Rees each modified it, and it became the structure that is today Ann's Eyewear Boutique, one of two 1904 structures extant.

Twin Falls needed a post office because:

The postmaster in Shoshone sent the mail to Twin Falls in a separate bag via the Rock Creek Stage and it was dumped on the counter at the Perrine and Burton Store where everybody helped himself to mail.

—Anna Hansen Hayes

Sometimes someone would not get a letter on the stagecoach on time so they would hire dad [Albert Urie] *to catch up to the stage on horseback and deliver the letter.* —Carl Urie (2001)

In September Harley O. Milner opened Twin Falls's first post office at his Twin Falls Lumber Company on Third Avenue at Third Street S (now Floyd Lilly Company). The mail was picked up at 9 A.M., arrived by stage at 3 P.M., and Twin Falls's first postmaster separated the mail into pigeon holes. But the booming town kept Mr. Milner so busy with his lumber business that his wife took over his post office duties. Her salary, based on the postage of two cents per letter, amounted to sixteen dollars the first month.

With the growing town her salary increased to eighty-seven dollars a month—a fortune! But with her family to raise, Mrs. Milner was also too busy to run the business, and the inconveniently located post office would move back to Main Avenue next to the Perrine and Burton Store and from there to the Perrine Hotel annex.

A city park got the townsite's first trees. The Townsite Company set aside parcels for a civic center, two schools, and a city park with half of its area designated for a high school and a courthouse. Hoops Construction Company grubbed and leveled the park's acreage. In the Willis Brothers' freight wagon from Shoshone came sturdy little elm trees to plant all around the periphery of the park and also other eastern species to landscape the rest of the area. When the townsite survey was completed in the fall, John E. Hayes's crew carried water to the saplings from the town's well by Rock Creek.

> *It was he* [James A. Waters] *who laid out the arrangement of tree planting in the Twin Falls City Park and actually set out these trees.*
>
> —James Albert Waters's Obituary,
> *The Twin Falls County Daily News*, 24 October 1928

Farmer/dairyman/nurseryman James A. Waters came to Twin Falls from Wisconsin by way of Yakima, Washington, to homestead 160 acres. The farmhouse he built on Falls Avenue E was the first house between the townsite and Perrine's Blue Lakes. Waters imported trees and shrubs from Shoshone and Hagerman and landscaped most of the residential lots and schoolyards as well as the park. (Some of the town's oldest trees are said to be "Waters's trees.") Waters would plant thousands of acres of orchard around the valley, mostly apples. He and I. B. Perrine would both win gold medals at World's Fair expositions.

The Townsite Company granted building sites around the park to all denominations of churches. In the spring of 1905 the Methodists and the Episcopalians would organize, the Baptists would build the first church in Twin Falls in May, and the first St. Edward's Catholic church would hold its first mass. The Presbyterians would organize in August, and the First Christian Church would organize in November 1905. The Church of Jesus Christ of Latter Day Saints would establish a branch of the Cassia Stake in 1907.

The first all-faiths Sunday School was held in the summer of 1904 by Blanche (Mrs. Fred) Ramsey, a Presbyterian, who found shade for it under the willows by Rock Creek. Mrs. Emma Clouchek started a Bible study class. The first minister to come to Twin Falls was Rev. Henry W. Parker, a Methodist from Shoshone.

That autumn the town had enough school children to warrant a schoolhouse.

> [The new schoolhouse] *can be used as a hall until such time as the various denominations erect their churches . . . Religious services are held twice a month.* —The Twin Falls News, 28 October 1904

A school committee formed to collect public subscriptions on the streets, and within one hour they had collected $600. Because the committee planned to build a temporary schoolhouse, they did not want to use one of the two locations that had been set aside for permanent schools. The Townsite Company allowed the use of two lots on the corner of Third Avenue and Third Street E (site of today's Covenant Bible Church behind the city hall).

> *This committee was to have charge of the building so long as it was used for school purposes, after which they were to sell it for the best price . . . and distribute the money to the contributors.*
>
> —Mareda Wright, librarian (2002)

Construction of the wood-framed schoolhouse began in October. When the building was near completion, the townsfolk engaged it for a Thanksgiving dance and party. When the schoolhouse was finally completed in December, sixty pupils were ready to enroll, but they would have to wait until 3 January for the desks to arrive. Also, there was no teacher. John E. Hayes (who earlier that year had met Anna Hansen whose father was a former Cassia County superintendent of schools) got the new superintendent of schools, Prof. H. H. Thornton, to fill in.

A children's Christmas party was planned to fill the empty schoolhouse. One day before the party, Sam Hamilton and Fred Eickhoff went to the South Hills to find a traditional evergreen tree for the festivity. Somehow they came back with an 8-foot sagebrush. After the party committee's shock and anger wore off, they accepted it as appropriate and decorated the sagebrush "tree" with tinsel and strings of popcorn. At least a hundred children and parents went to the schoolhouse to celebrate Christmas. The carols they sang were accompanied by Hortense Perrine at Blanche Ramsey's organ. Charlie Tripp put on Dr. Clouchek's great fur overcoat and cap and

SAGEBRUSH
CHRISTMAS TREE 1904

played Santa Claus, telling the children of his fine team of twenty-four big jackrabbits togged out in silver harness set off with dozens of bells. That first sagebrush-and-jackrabbit Christmas in Twin Falls would long be remembered . . . and the sense of humor of those first settlers would become legend.

The New Town Got the News

Important developments were unfolding Out West in Idaho. Two men from Salt Lake City, Charles Diehl and O. H. Barber, started to publish a weekly, *The Twin Falls News*, in a little building at 155 Main W, and a town six months old had a newspaper. The *News*'s first issue on 28 October 1904 lauded the new town's growth:

> *. . . two general stores, 2 livery stables, 2 restaurants, 2 saloons, a lumber yard, brick yard, meat market, blacksmith shop, rooming house, and real estate office. Under construction: hotel and stone store buildings. Under consideration: a national bank, a millinery store. A physician and dentist are here.*

There was a Young's General Store on Second Avenue E near Bassett's livery stable and saloon. There was a Parker Rooming House. The national bank referred to was the First National Bank of Twin Falls, which its president I. B. Perrine organized in October to finance the promotional luxury hotel. The first physician was Henry W. Clouchek from Michigan who came west to practice in Elgin, Oregon, where he met and married Emma Olds and then brought her to Twin Falls. The first dentist was James M. Rogers from Milner. Other news was the first birth in Twin Falls, that of Blanche Harrah on 15 August 1904.

> *Twin Falls lost a "first" when Blanche Aloda Harrah Faretta died on September 28 of complications from a broken hip at the age of 97 . . . in Fresno, California.* —*The Times-News*, 9 October 2001

Historical Update: In May 1905 Wilbur Hill started *The Twin Falls Times* a block away from the *News* at 218 Main N, and a town one year old with a population of five hundred had two newspapers. The price of the *Times* was the same as the *News*: two dollars per year, but with free delivery. To put the *News* in touch with the world, the first telegraph arrived at Will Perrine's farmhouse on 27 July 1905, one day before the railroad's arrival in Twin Falls. Hill changed the name of his paper to *The Idaho Evening Times*.

Roy Read purchased the *News* in 1913, moved it into a corner of the Masonic Hall on Second Street at Second Avenue W, changed the name to *The Twin Falls Morning News*, and made it a daily paper. Roland Tofflemire and Emil Bordewick purchased Hill's *Evening Times*. These partners bought out the *Morning News* in 1937 and continued to publish both papers in the little corner of the Masonic Hall.

In this crowded space, an *Evening Times* reporter Gus Kelker and a *Morning News* reporter took turns using one desk. In 1939 Kelker wrote "The True Facts of How Magic Valley Was Named":

"Toff" had called the meeting [of five men, in a 9-by-12-foot office]. *At that time our valley was simply south central Idaho. Toff thought that smelled. He wanted a new name to play a prominent part in the advertising of the* Times *and the* News *and also in stories which would have to detail which part of Idaho the news came from. Scores of suggestions—*

even "Fertile Valley"—came to light and for discussion during the session. . . . Suddenly, he [Toff] *suggested "Magic Valley" and that was that.*

The Magic Valley comprises about ten thousand square miles in eight counties: Twin Falls, Cassia, Minidoka, Jerome, Gooding, Lincoln, Camas, and Blaine.

In 1942 Tofflemire and Bordewick dropped the morning paper and named the one afternoon paper *The Times-News*. With the opening of the new Masonic Hall on Blue Lakes Boulevard in 1945, the *Times-News* purchased the old Masonic building which still bears the newspaper's name on the façade. In 1970 the *Times-News* moved to its present location at the corner of Second Avenue and Third Street W.

The Town's Beginning Was Right on Schedule

By the end of 1904 the grubbing of the streets was finished, the sagebrush was raked into rows and burned. Main Avenue had board sidewalks. Seventy-five lots had homes—temporary shacks and tents until houses like the McCollum's could be built when the railroad reached Twin Falls the following summer.

> *Father* [W. B. Hoag] *had walled up a tent for our first home (everyone lived in these at first). The beds, which consisted of springs and mattresses and bedding, were turned up and fastened with straps to the sides of the tent in the daytime.* —Wanda Hoag Reed

Meanwhile, at least fifty freight wagons a day were bringing food and supplies, mostly lumber, from Shoshone. Depending on which ferry the freighters used, Charlie Walgamott's or Bert Perrine's, they took either the Shoshone

Road or the Blue Lakes Road. On the Twin Falls side of the river these became Shoshone Street and Blue Lakes Boulevard and converged at the northeast corner of the townsite with a post in the middle of the intersection. All this noisy traffic, added to the din of construction, made daylight hours in Twin Falls a hubbub. But at night, the town's three hundred residents fell asleep to the quiet roar of Shoshone Falls six miles away, hoping and praying that they would not have much longer to suffer the hardship and inconvenience of settling a new town in the desert.

Suggested Reading Available at the Twin Falls Public Library

- *Tribute to the Past,* Legacy for the Future, Donna Scott,* 1990
- *Magic Valley Stories,* CSI collection from Virginia Ricketts's class,* 6 volumes
- *Then and Now in Southern Idaho,* Virginia Ricketts,* 1998
- *Bucking the Tide,* H. J. Kingsbury,* 1949
- *Six Decades Back,* Charles S. Walgamott,* 1936

* Local Magic Valley authors

Chapter 4

Twin Falls Village, 1905–1906

A plain with houses, shacks, tents, prairie schooners, brick business block, all just set down on it. Not a tree big enough to cast a shadow. Sagebrush everywhere, but the jolliest, most enthusiastic crowd of people you ever saw, most of them well-dressed.

—Grace (Mrs. Joseph H.) Seaver, Twin Falls pioneer settler

Incorporation Took Less Than a Year

The town's population, which started with Hayes's survey crew of three in late April 1904, reached five hundred before twelve months had passed. A petition was signed by 165 men and presented to the Cassia County Commission, and on 13 April 1905 Twin Falls was incorporated as a village. The five trustees who met in the little frame schoolhouse and served without pay were Paul Bickel, chairman of the Board of Trustees and mayor, Robert McCollum, S. T. Hamilton, Fred Eickhoff, and F. D. Bradley. The only paid official was the marshal, Albert Snodgrass.

The jail was their first order of business, although Trustee Sam Hamilton thought a jail in a cave worked just fine. He wrote:

> *In the spring of 1905 a tunnel was driven from the east-side wall of Rock Creek for several feet for use as a jail. Only a few individuals were placed in it, and they were told to be careful, that sometimes rattlesnakes were found there. The door was intentionally left unfastened, and the officer had scarcely reached the rim rock of the canyon after jailing his prisoners until they broke through the door. When word was passed around describing the jail and its probable reptile contents, wrongdoers avoided this section of the country, and the local crime rate took a decided decline.*

This cave was on the north (east) wall of Rock Creek Canyon (just below the stockyards that now border the railroad). When the trustees learned that a federal law prohibited the housing of prisoners below the surface of the ground, a new jail had to be considered. In 1907, on the alley at 240 Second Avenue S, a new jail would be built measuring 20-by-24 feet with an office, a room for female prisoners, and a room with three steel cages.

> *A new jail was completed . . . mainly for housing drunks.*
>
> —Larry Quinn, historian (1996)

The Board of Trustees passed ordinances that provided for an annual liquor license fee of two thousand dollars, a tax levy of ten mills for a permanent schoolhouse, planting of trees and shrubs along streets, sprinkling of streets to keep the dust down, dog control, for prohibiting loose livestock, and for franchises. One franchise went to the People's Telephone Company to install switchboards. Another went to the Twin Falls Waterworks Company to lay mains in streets and public places to furnish water from the canal system to the villagers, for which the company was allowed to charge a rate of two dollars per 4-room house. A fifty-year franchise went to I. B. Perrine to provide electric power to the village. In other business, John Bergman charged the Board twenty dollars for the road he built to the town's dump (Rock Creek, near the railroad stockyards).

The Village Bustled with Business

> *Father had bought three lots on Third Avenue S for building a house. There were many land-seekers and they were begging for meals and places to stay, so my parents decided to build a hotel.*
>
> —Wanda Hoag Reed

In February 1905 W. B. and Harriet Hoag built a hotel with six sleeping rooms at 125 Third Avenue S (recently Vicker's parking lot) and named it the Waverly for a hotel in their Michigan hometown. All equipment came from Sears and Roebuck in Chicago by rail to the Shoshone terminal and from there in Mr. Hoag's freight wagon. His was among the hundred freight wagons a day that were then making the trip from Shoshone to Twin Falls. Mr. Hoag also hauled water daily to the hotel from Rock Creek until the Waterworks Company laid mains.

Mr. Hoag drew a piece of homestead land south of Twin Falls in an early drawing, and while he farmed, Mrs. Hoag ran the hotel "by remote control," according to daughter Wanda. The village population was growing so fast that she had to set up beds outdoors until more rooms were available. After the railroad came to Twin Falls in August bringing more roomers, additions were made to the Waverly: a second story with ten more sleeping rooms, a wide porch, and a balcony. For eight years "Mother" Hoag would do all the cooking—family style meals were twenty-five cents—and cleaning and washing. Her permanent guests would have clean linen once a week. In 1913 the Hoags would lease the Waverly and move to a new farm south of Kimberly.

With all that freight coming daily from Shoshone, the town needed a transfer company. William Warberg saw the need when he brought his family to Twin Falls in 1905. Warberg, born in Sweden, came to America in 1888. One of the jobs he held in this country was with a transfer company in Boise. In Twin Falls he found a partner, a team of horses and a wagon, and the office of the Miller and Warberg Transfer Company opened in the back room of Jerry Hunt's barber shop on the alley off Second Street S.

Early in 1905, German-born Harder F. (H. F.) Harder brought his family and bakery equipment from Cripple Creek, Colorado, via railroad to Shoshone and on to Twin Falls.

> *He was unable to financially survive two citywide fires and two devastating miners' strikes* [in Cripple Creek]. *He made the decision to make the best settlement he could with his creditors, and with a loan from a long-time friend, he headed west to find a better place to be in business and to raise a family.* —Fred D. Harder, son (1990)

Mr. Harder opened his bakery shop in May at 230 Second Avenue E (now a parking lot) and sold bread at three loaves for twenty-five cents or fourteen loaves for a dollar, pies for fifteen cents, cookies and donuts for fifteen cents a dozen. Harder became a village trustee in May 1906. That summer he opened a new store at 117 Main Avenue E under the name of C. Harder

Grocery and Bakery—"C" for wife Carrie to avoid Colorado creditors. His sturdy cement block building had the year 1906 on the upper façade, and perched on top was the name Harder in stone. (Today the Harder Building displays only the date.)

HARDER BUILDING 1906

Mr. Harder rented his vacated Second Avenue building to F. W. Havilech, the first coroner, undertaker, embalmer, and ambulance service. When the first death in Twin Falls occurred on 16 February 1905, the town did not yet have a coroner. William Spencer's daughter died of measles in their tent home, and eight days later his wife died. Harriet Hoag from the Waverly prepared Mrs. Spencer for burial, did the washing, baked bread, and took care of the surviving son while Mr. Hoag took Mr. Spencer to Shoshone to buy another coffin.

Herman S. Martin donated twenty acres for a cemetery on Kimberly Road at Eastland Drive. This was a concern of the newly formed Twin Falls Commercial Club. Three club members met with two officers of the Twin Falls Land and Water Company that owned the land on Kimberly between Eastland and Blue Lakes Boulevard, and they arranged for a 1-mile right-of-way to be tree-lined and fenced. Bodies were transferred from the old cemetery at Eastland and Elizabeth to the new Twin Falls Cemetery. (Today you will find there the graves and headstones of many Twin Falls pioneers.)

O. H. and Harry F. Allen from Boise built their Allen Mercantile of red brick in 1905 at the corner of Main Avenue and Second Street S. But there was a clerical mixup, and the name was later changed to the Idaho Department Store, called the "I.D." On the ground floor were clothing and drygoods; in the basement, groceries and "bargains."

> *I always kept a large flock of laying hens to keep us in groceries and other needed goods. . . .The Idaho Dept. Store was open on the side street to traffic and one could drive up to the door, unload your crated eggs with the help of a child, and lug them to the grocery store in the basement to be traded for whatever was needed.* —Pearl M. Rayl

The top floor was occupied by the Knights of Pythias and would serve as the "county courthouse" from 1907 until 1911. This favorite store (now the Idaho Youth Ranch Store) would be remembered for its big white scales by the elevator, the drinking fountain with icy-cold water, and the round money carriers that traveled on overhead wires (before pneumatic tubes). Across the street was the popular Blue Front Café.

Carlos Oliver (C. O.) Meigs ran one of the many freight lines between Shoshone and Twin Falls. In 1905 he opened the C. O. Meigs Implement Company at 227 Third Avenue S (now a vacant lot). Before settling in Twin Falls, C.O. and his brother came from Iowa by way of Wisconsin and South Dakota to Idaho, and at Rocky Bar they milled lumber for the mines. Later, C.O. worked for Gov. Frank Gooding as overseer in his sheep business. In 1902 Meigs left Idaho with a consignment of sheep for the eastern market. Going through Michigan his train was wrecked and C.O. was taken to a hospital in Ann Arbor. The attending physician was a young intern named Henry W. Clouchek (and now we know who talked the doctor into coming west to become Twin Falls's first physician). Meigs would serve as acting mayor in 1911 and would be duly elected for the 1913–1915 term.

> *Early Fourth of July parades were distinguished for their length if for nothing else. Every implement company entered all its hay racks, binders, mowing machines, and plows to be mixed in with the cows and horses.* —Twin Falls High School Student Publication, 1944

The farmers Meigs served had a problem with rabbits. Jackrabbits ate alfalfa, grain, gardens, and orchards; in 1913 half the ravaged orchards would have to be almost entirely replaced. From time to time the farmers held jackrabbit drives. The critters were driven into a corral where Rock Creek joins the Snake River and were often clubbed to death. Many jumped off the rim into the canyon to escape.

> *500 men wanted to assemble promptly at 9:30 on Friday, Dec. 18 and take part in the great rabbit drive and coyote round-up. . . . Shot guns only allowed. Ladies are cordially invited. We want every man and boy in this drive that can possibly be there. Free lunch at the round-up. All business houses in Filer have agreed to close.*
>
> —Poster in the Twin Falls County Historical Society Museum

Jackrabbits were one problem for the farmers, the weather was another.

It turned bitter cold. Before the winter was over, the temperature had dropped to 40 below zero. . . . I used to look across the unblotted snow with no mark of any kind except two white haystacks which the rabbits had undermined until they looked like huge mushrooms.

—Annie Pike Greenwood, homesteader and author

They had severe weather back in those days—lots of snow, very cold and also very hot temperatures. I like to watch the weather reports for the records. It is amazing to me how many of those old records are still holding up.

—Jean Duffek-Nutsch

The Railroad Arrived in 1905 to a Celebration

A railroad through Twin Falls was as important to the growing town as it was to its agricultural community. I. B. Perrine's Investment Company guaranteed 6 percent of the cost of building the Oregon Shortline Railroad from Minidoka to Buhl, and the railroad company put up a guarantee bond. The bond would never have to be called in for interest as the railroad would pay for itself in freight charges and settlement.

The Oregon Short Line Company (a Union Pacific line) started construction in 1905 near Burley, and the railroad arrived in Twin Falls on 28 July. Members of the Twin Falls Commercial Club then traveled as far east as Pocatello inviting people from all the towns along the way to come on the first passenger train, and it arrived at the new depot on 7 August loaded with passengers. Other people rode in from as far west as Three Creek, from Rock Creek to the south, and Shoshone to the north until five thousand people crowded Twin Falls to celebrate Railroad Day.

Lars P. Larsen [23-year-old cowboy] *rode in from Rock Creek on a horse to witness the arrival of the first passenger train on August 7, 1905.*

—Gus Kelker, journalist

H. F. Harder was in charge of a community barbecue that was started the night before in a pit dug on the corner of Main and Shoshone (where Dunken's Drafthouse presently sits). "Two barrels of lemonade were made from two dozen lemons," and on that hot, sunny day, anything wet—however weak—was appreciated by the multitudes. Horse races, all kinds of races, were held. There was a pie-eating contest and there were fireworks. The highlight of the day was a baseball game between the Twin Falls Irrigators and the Pocatello Indians. Amid the celebrations, a platform was erected in front of the Perrine Hotel, then under construction, for speeches by no less dignitaries than Idaho Senator William B. Heyburn and Twin Falls Trustee S. T. Hamilton.

Historical Update: The railroad paid for itself, but Twin Falls paid a price. The corridor along Minidoka Avenue, which was presumed for residential use because of its lovely view of Rock Creek Canyon, was preempted by the railroad. South Park would never be "Knob Hill." A disappointed Paul Bickel resigned as mayor on 10 September 1906 and left Twin Falls. Named for him were the first permanent brick schoolhouse and a baseball field: Bickel School, which opened that month, and Bickel Field, now Latham Motors parking lot. Paul Bickel would return later to Twin Falls to be its city engineer.

Outdoor Entertainment Was Popular

John E. Hayes organized and managed the Twin Falls Irrigators baseball team in the spring of 1905. His team competed against the Burley Ditch Diggers, the Shoshone Gladiators, the Minidoka Miners, and other more distant teams. The Twin Falls team prevailed against Albion 16–15 in a home game, but in its first away game the Irrigators lost 10–6 to the Pocatello Indians. In the rematch between those two teams that was staged for Railroad Day, sweet revenge was denied the Irrigators as they went down again to the Indians, 6–5. The newspaper reported: "The Indians batted and ran as though the sheriff were after them."

A group of ten musicians formed a Twin Falls Band in 1905 to entertain the village at parades and in the park.

It is the second oldest continuously-performing municipal band in the Rocky Mountain West. Montana's Great Falls Band that goes back to perhaps the late 1880s is the oldest. Some eastern bands are even older. —Paula Sinclair, Twin Falls City Band Programmer, 2001

A Halloween festival in the fall of 1905 became Twin Falls's first fair on the corner of Shoshone and Second Avenue N (now the site of the Elks Lodge). Fruit and garden produce that won gold medals at the World's Fair were exhibited by I. B. Perrine. Farm families would wait eleven years to get a Twin Falls County Fair at its Filer location.

Rock Creek Yielded a Typhoid Epidemic

When settlement of Twin Falls began in 1904, Rock Creek was the abundant source of water for drinking and all other uses. Jesse Willis hauled water in barrels from the creek for fifty cents a barrel. When the creek went dry that fall, people dug wells.

First wash the dishes, then the baby, then the counters and mop the floor, then, if it is cold enough, water the flowers—they bring comfort and cheer. —Mrs. John Pierce, pioneer

Late that fall, the Twin Falls Waterworks Company pumped water from a Rock Creek well to a tank for the town's supply. The tank was intended to be temporary until water could be supplied to villagers through the company's mains fed by the canals. The canals began to receive water from Milner Dam on 1 March 1905, but the town grew faster than mains could be laid, and use of the tank was extended.

Fortunately Rock Creek is an unpolluted stream and will always carry an abundant supply of water so that all danger of shortage is eliminated. —*The Twin Falls News*, 5 June 1905

Waste, which had to go some place, was carried by pipe straight back to Rock Creek. Not so sure of the *News*'s cheerful statement, the Homeless Twenty organized the Twin Falls Commercial Club on 11 July "to look into the water situation." That fall, typhoid fever hit the settlement in the Rock Creek Canyon. Ambulances of "spring wagons drawn by broncos" brought up the sick to a restaurant on Second Avenue S that was outfitted as a hospital by Allen Mercantile with Mrs. Harry Allen in charge.

The Health Commission was alarmed by a report that a number of young gentlemen were feigning sickness and were warned that they would be ducked in Rock Creek and be made to drink creek water if they did not be good. —*The Twin Falls News*, 5 October 1905

This creek is a sewer now and always will be.
—*The Twin Falls News*, 18 May 1906

The beset village people demanded water from the irrigation canals. The Twin Falls Land and Water Company created a system that sent the water through settling ponds and then by gravity to the town's hydrants. This system would suffice until 1907 when screens would be so worn or broken that the canal water would bring little fishes through faucets into homes.

Prompted by the outbreak of typhoid, Doctors Clouchek, T. O. Boyd, and W. F. Pike created a Health Commission. Several doctors and a number of little hospitals were already established by late 1905, but the typhoid epidemic showed the need for a large central hospital. In June 1906 Doctors Boyd and Pike incorporated the Twin Falls Hospital Association with capital of $25,000 raised by Mark Murtaugh, the assistant manager of the TFL&WC. The hospital association built a 25-bed hospital near the corner of Third Avenue and Third Street W (now the post office parking lot). This "Boyd" Hospital would open in 1907 with five physicians. Dr. Boyd would open a school of nursing in 1911.

The Perrine Hotel Was a Triumph in the Desert

The typhoid epidemic was brought under control, and 1905 closed happily with the opening of the fabulous Perrine Hotel.

. . . the most modern and luxuriously furnished hotel in Idaho. Long distance phones in all the rooms, steam heated throughout, electric lights, private and public baths, and large free sample rooms.
—*The Twin Falls News*, December 1905

George Sprague supervised the hotel's construction on the corner of Main Avenue and Shoshone S. The 3-story hotel, designed by architect James H. Richardson, was built of lava rock from Shoshone and concrete bricks molded in Joe Dietrich's special machine in Rock Creek Canyon. Sprague, also the hotel's owner, first named his hotel The Kimberly for Peter Kimberly of the

TFL&WC. Mr. Kimberly died before completion of construction and Sprague changed the name to the Perrine Hotel (which was only fitting since Mr. Perrine would not let the town be named for him).

On 19 December 1905 was the Grand Opening of the Perrine Hotel with its open courts, conservatory, crystal chandeliers, uniformed bellboys, and a dining room which offered a choice of dinners: prime ribs of beef, roast leg of lamb, corned beef and cabbage, or roast chicken, with all the trimmings for fifty cents. On the two upper floors were fifty bedrooms—twenty with private baths—and four sample rooms.

> *An up-to-date hotel is crowded with city people all the time. Cowboys ride along the streets, and saddle horses are hitched at curbstones.*
>
> —Grace Seaver

Every day, from two to five hundred strangers came to town doubling its population and crowding the Perrine Hotel. At least one, Walter R. Priebe, slept on the floor in a sleeping bag and paid the full $1.25 room fee; rooms with private baths were $3.00. Sleeping space was at a premium, and Twin Falls's first druggist E. B. Williams, who became the hotel's manager, rented out a double bed-in-the-wall and two mattresses on the floor.

Businesses and offices occupied part of the hotel's first floor. I. B. Perrine moved the offices of his Jerome-Twin Falls Stage and his Twin Falls Investment Company into the hotel. The Investment Company's manager, Thomas Robertson, was George Sprague's brother-in-law and partner in the insurance business; these two men moved their agency into the Perrine Hotel.

At the rear of the hotel was the generating plant of I. B. Perrine's Electric Power Company. Using a threshing machine to pump water from Rock Creek through two thousand feet of pipe, an Edison bipolar generator produced thirty-five kilowatts of electricity. One hundred volts of direct current lit up the hotel and four village blocks in three directions from dusk to dawn. This generator would operate until 1907 when the power plant at Shoshone Falls would go on line.

Early on, Mr. Sprague's deluxe promotional hotel needed financing. That was provided in January 1905 when, with $25,000 in capital stock, I. B. Perrine incorporated the First National Bank of Twin Falls of which he was president. A temporary, wooden bank building for general banking was constructed next to Perrine's Investment Company's temporary shack-office. In 1906 a permanent First National Bank Building went up on the corner of Main and Shoshone E (now Key Bank). Where there was any kind of need connected with his irrigation project, Bert Perrine provided for it; of his many businesses, none bore the name of this modest man.

An earthquake in 1906 broke many of the hotel's wide glass windows. (An earthquake and fire on the West Coast that year destroyed San Francisco.)

1906 Claimed Four Firsts

Twin Falls volunteer firemen got a firehouse at the corner of Shoshone and Third Avenue N. The two volunteer fire department companies of twenty men each also got two hose carts, with five hundred feet of new rubber, at $110 each. Water was supplied by hydrants fed by gravity from the canals.

VOLUNTEER FIREMEN 1906

Bickel School on Second Avenue at Sixth Street E, the first permanent schoolhouse, opened in September 1906 to 130 students. With enrollment anticipated to climb to five hundred the next year, this steam-heated brick schoolhouse had thirteen classrooms and an assembly hall. Two-thirds of the pupils came from the country, and the school system was centralized to provide "equal opportunity for city and farm children."

> *Twin Falls District boasted the first central rural school in the state and blazed the way for centralizing schools. . . . The rural experiment proved successful and became the forerunner of similar systems.*
>
> —Mareda Wright

Rural kids four miles out were brought in by bus. A school bus was a horse-drawn wagon with a canvas top, long benches on either side for thirty children, straw on the floor and heated rocks or bricks to keep feet warm. Many drivers were farmers who put the horses in "the barn" at Bickel School for the day.

SCHOOL BUS DRIVER:
LEONARD EMERSON, AGE 15

> *We all learned to work and play together and fitted children to take their place in the community. We weren't rich but we didn't know it. You were taught to live within your means. If you couldn't pay for something, you learned to wait until you had the cash to pay for it and probably by that time you really didn't need it or want it.*
>
> —Emily Tverdy, homesteader

The Colorado Milling and Elevator Company, which had four companies in Colorado, established the Twin Falls Milling and Elevator Company on Minidoka Avenue off Shoshone Street S.

> *The Twin Falls Milling and Elevator Company was one of the largest milling and storage operations between Denver and Portland.*
>
> —Ron Stanley (2002)

Under the management of L. L. Breckenridge, the Twin Falls flour mill developed a variety of flours. It made a bakery flour called "Idahome,"a biscuit flour called "Twinida," a cake flour called "Shone-Mist," and an all-purpose flour called "Pike's Peak"—a reminder of the Colorado firm.

The mill developed a cake flour called "Duncan Hines," which is still made under the same name by another company.

—Miriam B. Breckenridge (1990)

In the 1930s the local flour company would build bean elevators nearby and would buy and sell beans. Gradually operations would be curtailed, and the last of Twin Falls's flour company would be sold in the early 1960s.

Historical Update: All that remains at the site of the 1906 Twin Falls Milling and Elevator Company are the six 1909 grain elevators and the 1912 brick warehouse behind them on Second Street S. The impressive warehouse, which today is owned by Ron Stanley and Cliff Gambrel, is on the National Register of Historic Places.

Photographer Clarence E. Bisbee came to Twin Falls in 1906 by the flip of a coin: tails, Fort Worth, Texas; heads, Idaho. Bisbee and Charles Diehl had met in photography school in Illinois. After Diehl started the *News* in 1904, he asked Bisbee to come and photograph "Twin Falls civilization" to show easterners that there was more here than sagebrush and coyotes. Bisbee set up his studio in a tent on Main Avenue, and for seventeen months he used ditch water for developing film, for bathing and laundry; he got his drinking water from a nearby undertaking parlor. Clarence would marry his Jesse in 1910, and four years later he would build a fine studio at Second Avenue and Second Street E.

Bisbee would photograph Twin Falls from 1906 to 1939. His outstanding collection, much of it to be housed in the Twin Falls Public Library's Idaho Room, would document the infancy and growth to maturity of a little outpost built in Idaho by the Snake River and named for its twin falls.

CLARENCE BISBEE

Suggested Reading Available at the Twin Falls Public Library

- *Territorial Centennial Twin Falls County 1863–1963*
- *Growth of a City*, KLIX, 1952
- *Officials of Twin Falls*, 1905–1936
- *Tribute to the Past, Legacy for the Future*, Donna Scott,* 1990
- *A History of the Magic Valley*, Larry Quinn,* 1996
- *Those Pioneers*, Anna Hansen Hayes,* 1946
- *A Decade and One Year of Change*, A.O. (Gus) Kelker,* 1974
- *Idaho State Centennial: Local History 1890–1990*

*Local Magic Valley authors

Chapter 5

Twin Falls City and County, 1907–1914

A span of years when you could hear the ringing of hammers at all hours of the night and day. —Walter R. Priebe, jeweler

They would put their dishes in a washtub and carry them from one house to the other at threshing time, as neither of them had enough dishes to accommodate a threshing crew of twenty-four men. —Pearl M. Rayl

A New County and City After Just Three Years

By an act of the Idaho legislature, signed by Gov. Frank Gooding on 21 February 1907, Twin Falls County, third class, was split off of Cassia County. This was another project pushed by the Twin Falls Commercial Club. The first Twin Falls County commissioners elected were John F.

Hansen, L. E. Salladay, and Dr. George Crocker. The commissioners held their meetings upstairs in the Idaho Department Store until 1911 when the new Twin Falls County Courthouse was completed.

Along with the rapidly growing rural community, the Twin Falls village population grew to fifteen hundred in 1907. With over one thousand inhabitants the town qualified for status of city, second class, and H. F. Harder circulated a petition for that status. After Harder obtained the required signatures of three-fifths of the voters, the village Board of Trustees passed the resolution, and on 15 March 1907 the Village of Twin Falls became the City of Twin Falls. An election was held in the firehouse where 130 men cast votes to elect five city council members. Councilman Fred A. Voigt of the Twin Falls Land and Water Company was chosen the first mayor of the city. The first Twin Falls City Council passed an ordinance that made it unlawful to ride a horse in the city limits at more than six miles per hour; the fine, up to one hundred dollars. The next year, the City Council set a speed limit of eight miles per hour because of the dust raised by a growing number of automobiles. Also in 1907 a new sewer system was installed and the Great Shoshone and Twin Falls Power Company's plant went on line.

Civic Affairs Bustled

Bickel School, overcrowded with an enrollment of eight hundred, had its first graduation in 1908 for a class of eight seniors. The next year, the new Lincoln School at Second Avenue and Eighth Street W opened to twelve hundred students. The Twin Falls School District had fourteen school busses bringing students in from four miles out. All of the other twenty-one school districts in Twin Falls County had little 1- and 2-room schools.

Bond elections in 1908 provided $10,000 for walks, culverts, and bridges, and another $10,000 for the Fire Department's new station—the first one burned down. The new station was built in front of the jail at 240 Second Avenue S at a cost of $5,516. The volunteer firemen got a chief, J. P. Taggart, with a salary of $15 per month, and a new steam fire engine that cost more than the station at $5,986. The city's chief of police, W. G. Thompson, had two patrolmen.

The Twin Falls County Commission resolved not to renew existing liquor licenses in February 1909. In the November elections that year, the county went dry and was one of the earliest counties to do so before the passage of

STEAM FIRE ENGINE 1908

the 18th Amendment in 1919 that began an era of "Prohibition." In 1911 the Twin Falls City Council passed an ordinance prohibiting the sale of alcoholic beverages in the city.

In 1910 street paving began downtown, Rock Creek got a bridge, and the Masonic Hall was constructed. By then, Twin Falls had twelve secret and benevolent organizations of which the Masons was one. Flag Day was celebrated at Shoshone Falls where bleachers were provided and a band stand was erected for a concert by the City Band. Among the speakers was Ezra Meeker who was heading east in his ox-drawn covered wagon to establish commemorative markers along the Old Oregon Trail. Meeker had made the trip to Oregon as a young man in 1852, and this was his way of raising interest in the preservation of the historic Oregon Trail.

On 10 October 1911 the last covered wagons arrived in Twin Falls—three of them, each with two teams of horses and two extra horses. The extended McCracken family from Kansas traveled across that state, Colorado, Wyoming, and Idaho on roads that followed the railroad. Railroad people were friendly and threw them coal and let them water their horses. The emigrants bought butter and milk at farms along the way. They saw Indians all across Wyoming and at the Fort Hall Reservation in Idaho.

> *Friends told them, "You're crazy to make the trip. If Indians don't get you, the Mormons will." The Old West wasn't that far back when your own grandparents came out.*
>
> —Vernon McCracken, Twin Falls (2001)

In April 1911 two thousand shade trees were planted along Blue Lakes Boulevard. That year Mr. Perrine built a toll bridge that replaced his ferry, and construction of the Twin Falls County Courthouse (C. Harvey Smith, architect) was completed. The new Twin Falls High School next to the Courthouse was finished by contractor William C. (W. C.) Reed the following year, the junior high school would be added in 1919.

> *The best equipped high school in the Northwest. Dances were held regularly in the large auditorium. Some very famous people performed on stage from time to time.* —Territorial Centennial

COUNTY COURTHOUSE 1911 TWIN FALLS HIGH SCHOOL 1912, & JUNIOR HIGH 1919

Twin Falls's first decade of remarkable civic progress drew to a close with a special Waterworks Committee seeking new water sources and drawing plans for a new municipal water system.

Commerce Was Unconstrained

When the irrigation project got underway in 1903, two local cattlemen supplied the construction crews with beef: Frank J. Terrill, foreman for the Russell Bradley Cattle Company in the Artesian area (Murtaugh Lake), and Robert Brose who worked for the Shoesole outfit on Rock Creek. In 1906 Brose opened his Twin Falls Meat Company market at 209 Main Avenue E and had an abattoir (slaughterhouse) in Rock Creek Canyon south of town. Terrill started the Independent Meat Market at 147 Main Avenue W (now Rudy's) and also built an abattoir in the canyon. In 1910 Carl Jungst acquired a third meat market at 240 Main Avenue N. These three men merged their companies and formed the Independent Meat Company.

First located at 124 Second Avenue S in 1907, the Consolidated Wagon and Machine Company moved in 1909 to its new building at 202 Main Avenue N (now Cain's). Under manager Lester T. Wright, the third floor was used for wagon repair, the second floor was for displays, and the first floor was for assembled wagons and tractors, and for threshing machines when they became available. The new building had thirty-two stoves in which the workers built fires as heat was needed, until the a steam boiler was installed in the basement.

Great caution was taken against fire. —Robert Adamson

At 210 Second Avenue S in 1907 (now the Salvation Army's Thrift Store) stood The Farmers Blacksmith Shop founded by Herbert Gale and E. E. (Ernest) Krengel. Mr. and Mrs. Krengel emigrated on the Oregon Trail in 1852 from Iowa to California where son Charles was born. From there they went to British Columbia, then to Moscow, Idaho, where Charles grew up and attended college to study engineering. The family's last move was to Twin Falls. The blacksmith shop became the Krengel family business with the father shoeing horses, sharpening plow shares, and repairing wagons and buggies while the son ran the hardware section. After E.E. died of typhoid in 1912, Charles expanded the machine shop to employ seven forgers to manufacture his inventions, such as the sagebrush grubber.

SAGEBRUSH GRUBBER

The sagebrush grubber was a horse-drawn, 2-wheeled machine with arms that held two cutters which ran under the sagebrush and cut it off well underground. —Pearl M. Rayl

A. M. Sande started the Twin Falls Feed and Ice Company. Born in Norway, Sande arrived in Idaho in 1897 to work as a sheepman for Rogerson-

MacRae Sheep Company. Sande went into business for himself in 1907 to provide feed and ice for the Twin Falls merchants and residents.

> *Uncle was known and respected as a man of his word. A bond was established in the days when a handshake was a legal contract.*
>
> —Einar Sande (1990)

In southern Idaho's very cold winters, thick ice would form on a large pond near Rock Creek north of Addison Avenue. Using a handsaw, Sande harvested the ice in blocks, then stored them in sawdust- or coal-dust-filled sheds and dispensed them throughout the year. In later years with a few warm winters, no ice would form on the pond for blocks. By 1930, ice-making machines would replace saw labor. For forty years Gene Larsen would drive Sande's ice wagon drawn by the familiar pinto horse. Larsen would deliver thousands of pounds of ice a day to unlocked houses, use ice tongs to put the blocks in each ice box, collect the money or coupon, and leave. (Sande's original ice wagon is preserved at the Twin Falls County Historical Society Museum and Visitor Center on West Addison near Curry Crossing.)

Pioneer sheepmen Andrew Rogerson and John MacRae, both Scotsmen, opened their Rogerson Hotel for business in December 1908.

> *The sign read: The Rogerson European Hotel—First Class Café. . . . The architect was the well-known C. Harvey Smith.*
>
> —Curtis Steen and Donna Scott (1990)

Steam heat, hot and cold running water, telephones and call bells were the features of this luxury hotel on the corner of Main Avenue and Second Street E. The second and third floors held the hotel's office and a lobby, eighty-five bedrooms, private and public baths, and seven large sample rooms. The ground floor of this handsome brick hotel—known as "The Nordling"—was reserved for businesses. The Nordling sisters from Chicago opened a store with "ladies' stuff:" hats, stationery, books, and things. Bonham and Peters opened the Racket and Novelty Store. C. C. Wilson's Lobby Cigar Store became headquarters for baseball and other sports fans. Meyer and Company Outfitters employed fourteen people and had a mail order business.

Louis Benoit, who spoke only French, and his sons Albert and Harry arrived in 1905 from Wisconsin and opened the Blue Lakes Bottling and Spring Water Plant in 1908. At 545 Shoshone Street S (now the Depot Grill) the Benoits bottled ginger ale, soda water, and spring water brought from Blue Lakes.

> *My dad* [Albert Benoit] *had a wagon full of barrels and pulled by a 4-horse team. He made two trips a day to Blue Lakes and had lunch every day with the Perrines from whom he purchased the water.*
>
> —Robert Benoit (1990)

They obtained Twin Falls's first Coca-Cola franchise in 1908, then they expanded their enterprise by building apartments and movie theaters. In 1913 the first airplane was brought to Twin Falls in sections on a railroad car, unloaded at Benoit's bottling plant, and put together; from there it took off.

> *Tojito "Tom" Koto, like so many other Japanese men at the turn of the century, came to the U. S. A. to work on the railroad.*
>
> —Tom Koto, son (1990)

In Weiser, Tom Koto's first restaurant was "not so good." In 1908 he came to Twin Falls and opened a restaurant on Main Avenue S in a building next to the construction site of the Twin Falls Bank and Trust. This time business was good, and Tom would remain at that location for twelve years.

Richard E. Bobier came to Twin Falls in 1908 to work in construction. Bobier was the brick mason for the Twin Falls Canal Company Building, which was completed when that company was incorporated in 1909. On the corner of Second Street W diagonally across from that building, the

Masonic Hall was completed the next year with Bobier the brickmason. Bobier and his son A.D. "Tony" formed the Bobier Construction Company, and together they would build the Sande Building in 1916, the Mountain States Tel and Tel Building and second First Baptist Church on Shoshone Street E, the Twin Falls Public Library, Radio Rondevoo, and others. R. E. Bobier would serve as mayor of Twin Falls for six years, from 1927 to 1933.

MASONIC BUILDING 1910

His contributions to the domestic scene have been small apartment houses; the brick work on several homes includes fireplaces.

—Helen Lamb (1990)

The new Light and Power Company Building provided lots of office space.

The Great Shoshone & Twin Falls Water Power Company, the Twin Falls Water Power Company, the Twin Falls Salmon River Land & Water Company, and the Twin Falls Northside Land & Water Company moved their offices this week from the north wing of the Hotel Perrine [to the new building.]

—*The Twin Falls News*, 11 December 1908

The Twin Falls Land and Water Company and the Twin Falls Investment Company (which would cease operation the next year) also took offices in the Light and Power Company Building at 164 Main Avenue N (now Peach Tree Creek Restaurant). There the Twin Falls Railway Company opened its office in 1913 to manage its short-lived electric train between the city and Shoshone Falls. In 1916 the Idaho Power Company would incorporate and have its headquarters in this building for fifty years.

The pounding of the wooden mallet against the flat sheets of tin and the squeak of the 8-foot brake—which bends corners into the metal . . .

—Jennifer Kauth (1990)

Harry Brizee learned the sheet metal trade in San Jose, California. Brizee came to Twin Falls in 1909 and bought a sheet metal manufacturing shop at Main Avenue and Third Street E. Harry first named the shop Twin Falls Sheet Metal but soon changed the name to Brizee Metal Works and moved it to the 100 block of Second Street E.

McCornick Company built the Twin Falls Bank and Trust Building in 1910.

> *Designed by C. Harvey Smith who also designed the Twin Falls County Courthouse.* —Carol D. Huether (1990)

For three years W. S. McCornick and Company, Bankers of Salt Lake City, had a branch bank at 138 Main Avenue S (now Tesori). In 1908, with plans to expand in the future, the company purchased Perrine and Burton's strategic corner at Main and Shoshone S for $23,000; Silas and Will Perrine and William Burton retired and returned to farming. When construction began, the bank incorporated under a new name: Twin Falls Bank and Trust Company. (Today the handsome building is on the National Register of Historic Buildings and is owned by the Wells Fargo Bank.)

TWIN FALLS BANK & TRUST 1908

Walter R. Priebe from Minnesota via Washington State arrived in Twin Falls with Antoine Guibert on 12 May 1908. The partners purchased a jewelry store at 128 Main Avenue W from J. G. Granger. Walter could then sleep in the aisle of his store rather than on the floor of the crowded Perrine Hotel, which still had guests sleeping in the lobby. The streets were not yet paved, and Walter "wiped dust off the glass cases hourly and shoveled mud out on wet days." In 1910 Walter Priebe moved his business into the new Twin Falls Bank and Trust Building with entrance on the Shoshone Street side.

Wedding guests and friends [of Elva, daughter of Bob and Alice McCollum] *caused a rush of gift-giving, and the complete stock of the newly-opened jewelry business was almost depleted.*

—James A. Priebe, son (1990)

Clarence Allen became the sixth licensed optometrist in Idaho on January 23, 1910. —Howard L. Allen, son (1990)

With a job waiting for him in Pocatello, Clarence Allen took the train from Missouri in 1910. A sound sleeper, he missed his stop and got off at American Falls. There he heard about a booming town not far to the west, and so he wound up in Twin Falls. Allen opened an optometry salon in the balcony of Priebe's jewelry store in the new bank building. But practice was sparse and Allen went into watch-making, jewelry repair, and hand engraving. In 1913 Clarence married Anna Anderson whose father Levi Anderson was one of Twin Falls's first concrete contractors.

The beautiful mission-style Justamere Hotel was designed by architect John Visser and constructed in 1910 at Fourth Avenue and Second Street N. This hotel with stucco and tile and big baroque gables contained thirty-three bedrooms and suites, a dining room to seat fifty, and a large cozy "living room" with a huge fireplace. (Today the Justamere is an office building that regularly wins the Business Landscaping Award.)

Sheepherders came to town and needed to sleep with their valuable dogs—Perrine Hotel said "No." —Jacob Arrington (1990)

From drought-ridden Oklahoma came "Jake" Arrington in 1911. He built housing in the 500 block of Second Avenue S where the sheepherders could sleep with their valuable sheep dogs. Across the street at the Twin Falls Athletic Park in Bickel Field, Jake ran a concession and peddled pop, candy, and popcorn to the fans.

Lawrence Clos opened Twin Falls's first permanent book and stationery store in 1912 on Shoshone Street W (behind the Magic Valley Bank

Building). In 1915 Clos would move to 121 Main Avenue W where, for forty-seven years, his store would dispense the textbooks provided by the state.

> *Clos was the only place the school books could be purchased, so September was an especially hectic time for the store.*
>
> —Betty Purves (1990)

We saw Twin Falls's first dray company, Warberg's, get established in 1905 with a team of horses and a wagon. William Warberg expanded the business with a second team of horses and a new partner, Carl Benson. The lumber companies—Twin Falls had seven by 1910—kept Warberg's Transfer Company busy, and Warberg soon had eight teams of horses and the first Buick truck in Twin Falls.

> *A friend asked Dad if he thought the automobile would ever take the place of horses. He replied, "No, horses are too much part of our economy."*
>
> —Zoe Ann Warberg Schaub (1990)

With the completion in 1913 of Warberg's new building on Shoshone Street S (next to the present Red's Trading Post), Twin Falls took pride in its first decade of remarkable commercial and economic growth.

Chapter 6

For Twin Falls: A Name and Electricity

I remember that he [I. B. Perrine] *was a very respected but humble man. I recall that the entire town wanted to name this city Perrine rather than Twin Falls, but he insisted that it not be named after him.*

—Roy Babbel and Timi Cantrell (1990)

How the Townsite Got a Name in 1904

Many towns take the names of their founders, many others are named for outstanding natural landmarks. A little railroad town established in 1882 twenty-five miles north of the magnificent Shoshone Falls of the Middle Snake River chose that landmark's name. I. B. Perrine chose the name of the second largest falls for his Twin Falls Land and Water Company (TFL&WC) in 1900, and this company gave the name to its townsite and to its Twin Falls Townsite Company in 1904. The first townsite plat was therefore filed under the name of Twin Falls, but—even with all its provenance—the name was not "chiseled in granite."

In April 1904 John E. Hayes and his crew were working on a survey west of the townsite when a traveler visited their camp. From him they learned that a group of independent promoters had chosen the name of Twin Falls for their settlement east of the townsite, on the freight and stage road that ran between Rock Creek and Shoshone Falls.

That night Hayes wrote a letter with this information to his boss Paul Bickel who was at his camp at Milner Dam. Since the visitor was on his way to Rock Creek, he delivered the letter to that post office the next day. The

Shoshone-Rock Creek Stage picked up the letter, took it to Shoshone, and from that post office the message went to Milner Dam.

Bickel quickly sent an engineer on horseback to Hayes's camp to relieve Hayes of the westside survey so he could begin the Twin Falls townsite survey. Instead, Hayes sped on the same horse to confer with Bickel because the required townsite company had not yet been formed. But there was no time to lose on formality—it was already late April—and Bickel put Hayes to work immediately on the townsite survey. As soon as four townsite blocks from the center of the section were surveyed, the plat was rushed to Milner for the signatures of Bickel and Martin DeLong and then on to Albion, seat of Cassia County. There the first filing of the Twin Falls townsite plat was made on 12 May 1904.

Hayes's crew continued diligently with the survey. On 16 June the TFL&WC finally incorporated the Twin Falls Townsite Company to administer its townsite. On that same day, I. B. Perrine incorporated his Twin Falls Investment Company to perk up the sluggish sales of Carey Act homestead land. Townsite lot sales were also slow, so in July the Townsite Company contracted with Perrine's Investment Company to sell town lots and parcels as well. Fourteen more townsite blocks were platted and then filed on 19 August. The Investment Company's promotion was creating a demand for lots. Hayes promised that the survey would be finished and all lots would be available for sale by 4 October, the deadline to beat the other town to the name of Twin Falls. The race was on.

On 4 October the draftsmen had the final plat of the entire square-mile townsite ready to file. The drive to Albion would be a long one, at best six and a half hours of very hard driving. George Bassett with the town's first livery stable had a team he would hire out for the critical dash. By round-about, relayed telephone messages, arrangements were made for the clerk at the recorder's office in Albion to be on duty—until midnight if necessary—whenever the papers arrived.

The trip began late, at 5:45 P.M., and off the team sped heading for Milner to get the signatures of Bickel and DeLong. The road was a combination of wide, choppy tracks produced by the canal construction equipment and dust a foot deep. There were no bridges over the laterals, and it was down, across, and up again at every trench. Milner was reached and the horses had a short rest while the names were signed. Then, on they sped through the sagebrush to the main road to Albion.

At 11:45 P.M. the tired team and driver stopped in front of the courthouse where a light shone in the recorder's office window. In those last few minutes of 4 October 1904 the final plat was recorded and the town of Twin Falls got its name "chiseled in granite."

Based on a story by Anna Hansen Hayes, 1946

Twin Falls Park Was a Power Company's Gift. The name of Twin Falls for one of the Snake River's cataracts was obvious before 1935, the year the Idaho Power Company dammed and diverted the south Twin to turn the turbines of a power plant. The remaining falls has a drop of 130 feet. On the south side of the falls is the 10-acre Twin Falls Park owned and maintained by the Idaho Power Company. Here are picnic tables, a boat ramp on the reservoir above the falls, and an interpretive overlook at the dam.

Three miles upriver from Twin Falls Park is the Hansen Bridge, and seven miles above that is the Murtaugh Bridge. These ten miles of the Snake River is called the "Murtaugh Reach." The part of the reach between the bridges has four exhilarating major rapids and is rated by kayakers as high as 5 on a scale of 1 to 6, depending on the flow. The final, calmer miles of the reach from below the Hansen Bridge to the Twin Falls Park boat ramp is popular with users of all kinds of watercraft.

How Twin Falls Got Electric Power in 1907

As it still affects tourists today, Shoshone Falls took Charlie Walgamott's breath away on that day he first saw it in 1875. Charlie immediately staked a claim on the south rim of the falls, and for the next several years he lived there dreaming of one day having a tourist business. Charlie married in 1879 and his wife joined him in his dream. When he saw the grade for the railroad that would come to Shoshone in 1883 bringing tourists among its passengers, Charlie moved his family to Shoshone. He made a partner of Joe Sullaway, a veteran stagecoach driver, and they staked a claim on the north side of Shoshone Falls. Together the partners hewed out a wagon road from the north canyon rim down to the river where, in a clearing above the falls, they set up a "first class hotel of tents:" nightly charge, one dollar. They also built a ferry above the falls between the two claims. Charlie and Joe were ready for the tourists.

WALGAMOTT'S TENT HOTEL

When the railroad finally arrived at Shoshone, the two men scheduled daily coach trips to their "resort." But flocks of tourists simply didn't materialize. For several weeks the hopeful partners made daily trips, even with empty coaches, to make it appear they had a successful business. Then the tourists came—in spurts—and the hostelers had difficulty accommodating thirty to forty people in bedding for ten or twelve. They did succeed in establishing their "Shoshone Road" that would continue to carry tourists, if by spells, for many years. Among the tourists were some wealthy and influential people.

One of Charlie's tourists who came that first year and was impressed with the falls was Charles H. Dewey of Omaha, Nebraska. Dewey made Charlie an offer on his southside claim, then wired W. A. Clark (who would become a senator) in Butte, Montana. Clark, Dewey, and his two Omaha law firm associates John A. Creighton and E .L. Stone, bought Charlie's southside claim in 1883. On the canyon rim overlooking Shoshone Falls they built, in 1886, the sumptuous Dewey Hotel with twelve bedrooms, dining room, kitchen, parlor, and bar. (This hotel would burn down in 1915 and never be rebuilt.)

Shoshone Falls became the center of a controversy. As early as 1879, studies were made concerning irrigation of the Snake River Plain, and irrigation was found to be feasible. Passage of the Carey Act in 1894 made an irrigation project a possibility with the construction of a dam in the Snake River Canyon. To ban such construction—and protect his investment at Shoshone Falls—Sen. W. A. Clark of Montana presented to Congress in 1898 a proposal for a national park preserve along that stretch of the canyon between The Cedars and the Blue Lakes. Congress tied up the land on both sides of the river in a congressional committee study.

Two years later, I. B. Perrine incorporated his Twin Falls Land and Water Company to contract with the state for his irrigation project, and his company and the governor of Idaho sent a delegation to Washington, D.C., to lobby Congress. In 1901 Congress opted for agriculture over a park preserve, and the tied-up land was released. The company's plans for irrigation from the Milner Dam site—and Perrine's plans for power from the Shoshone Falls site—went forward.

But there remained a "fly in the ointment." I. B. Perrine's associate in his power plant project was Harry L. (H. L.) Hollister, an agent of the Arnold Company of Chicago, which promoted the sale of land in the Salmon Tract. (The Arnold Company was in the building where Peter Kimberly had a corporate office.) The partners' Hollister Corporation was registered to construct a power plant at Shoshone Falls, but work got only as far as a coffer dam on the north side above the falls. Sen. W. A. Clark obtained an injunction and held up work for a year while he fought for title to Charlie's land on the north side of the falls. Clark lost his case, but in the delay, Hollister lost some of his backers.

New investors were found, and on 9 March 1904 Perrine and Hollister incorporated the Shoshone Falls Power Company. The company obtained the rights to their project so far done as well as the rights to the Twin Falls, Auger Falls, Upper and Lower Salmon Falls, and the Malad River at its confluence with the Snake River. Work resumed. The construction equipment that was required to tunnel through the solid rock was shipped by rail to Shoshone. From there it was hauled twenty-five miles across the desert by horse-drawn wagons to the rim rock above the plant site and then lowered to the canyon floor. A 440-foot tunnel that would direct water to the turbine was begun toward the lip of the falls.

Again the company ran out of money. This time the big investors were the Kuhn Brothers of Pittsburgh, Pennsylvania, whom Hollister knew since the Arnold Company also promoted the Kuhns' interests. On 26 January 1907 the Kuhns incorporated a third power company, the Great Shoshone and Twin Falls Water Power Company, to acquire the property rights of the bankrupt company and to assume its materials, construction contracts, and unfinished work. The power plant went on line in August 1907, and I. B. Perrine's old thirty-five kilowatt generator behind the Perrine Hotel in Twin Falls gave way to a new five hundred kilowatt unit. The "fly" was finally out of the "ointment." Nothing would come easily to I. B. Perrine who never gave up.

> *Agreement, March 1, 1908: Great Shoshone & Twin Falls Water Power Company, first, and City of Twin Falls, second. Good till August 1, 1911. (Renewed.)*
>
> *. . . to install 25 standard enclosed street lighting arc lamps . . . to maintain and operate, all night and every night . . . to furnish and supply electricity for power and for lighting purposes. City of Twin Falls agrees to pay . . . $6/mo. for each and every arc light so maintained and operated.*

Historical Update: The National Securities Corporation, a holding company, gathered the rights and interests of the several local power companies into a single operating company on 14 April 1914. The next year, the Idaho Power Company was incorporated after "mysteriously" gaining the final monopoly, and was in business in 1916. A judicial sale of the Shoshone Falls Power Plant was held on 28 February 1916, the purchaser was the Electric Investment Company, and in 1918 the plant was deeded to the Idaho Power Company. In 1929 the Idaho Supreme Court ruled against municipal power development, and the Idaho Power Company's virtual monopoly in the Magic Valley was cinched.

Shoshone Falls Park Was Started With a Gift. In the days before dams and power plants, Shoshone Falls was the upstream limit of the Snake River salmon runs. Today the salmon come no more, and in drought times, the

Shoshone Falls are no more. The volume of water at the falls is controlled for irrigation purposes by the several dams above it.

On the south side of Shoshone Falls is a 530-acre Shoshone Falls and Dierkes Lake Park complex owned by the city of Twin Falls. The falls are a major attraction in the West having a spectacular drop of 212 feet—that's 52 feet higher than Niagara Falls. Near the park's boat ramp above the falls are the remnants of the ferry operation started by Charlie Walgamott more than 120 years ago. For fifty-seven years this ferry ran, until 1940 when the toll was removed from the Perrine Bridge. When Clark, Dewey, Creighton, and Stone became rim-land owners in 1883, they held 68 acres. Mr. Frederick Adams and his wife Margaret Stone Adams of Omaha, Nebraska, purchased that property from the heirs in 1922, and in 1932 they gave it to the city as a Christmas present. In 1933 the state of Idaho donated another 270 acres to the park. Dierkes Lake Park was added in 1969.

German-born John Dierke came to Idaho in 1907 and worked with the Idaho Power Company after it was incorporated in 1916. While working around Shoshone Falls, he discovered a blind canyon through which ran a small creek. There John planted apple, cherry, and peach trees. After a few years, due to irrigation of the fields above, the small creek began to fill the canyon and John's trees were irrigated for him. Then, as the moisture in the fields seeped through the underlying porous lava rock, springs formed and the orchard began to flood.

> *In 1926 the lake wasn't completely full, but that summer John Dierke picked his first crop of peaches from a rowboat.*
>
> —Carol Mingo, CSI student

By 1927 the canyon was completely full of water creating Dierke's lake. John and his son Herb built a dock and a raft with a cable so kids could pull themselves across the lake to the big rocks, which were more daring for diving off than was the dock. This developed into a concession with six or seven rowboats, which rented for twenty-five cents, and a pop-and-candy stand. The entrance fee was ten cents per car (but kids came on their bicycles and could sneak in free). On Sundays there were boat races and picnics on blankets in the tall wild grass on higher ground under the remaining cherry trees.

After John died in 1954, Herb Dierke sold his 156 acres with lake to his partner Fred Foss who sold the property to the city of Twin Falls in 1969.

When added to the donations by the Adamses and the state of Idaho, plus the Britt acquisition of 35 acres in 1969, this brought the city park complex to a 530-acre total. As a condition of renewal of its license for its power plant on the north side of Shoshone Falls, the Idaho Power Company made a considerable financial contribution for improvements at the park site.

A trail now starts on the east side of the lake past the docks and winds around to the west side of the lake past the archery range and rock-climbing areas. The swimming areas have a sandy beach and a lifeguard in the summer. Other amenities are a concession stand, restrooms, covered picnic shelter, playgrounds, and fishing areas. This park complex is open daily year around from 7 A.M. to 9 P.M.; the fee is three dollars per car.

Historical Update: Annually since 1997, groups of as many as eighty local people including more than forty divers carry out trash from Dierkes Lake and Shoshone Falls Park. This yearly cleanup is sponsored by River Rat Toyz, Dive Magic, Fiesta Ole, and Swire Coca-Cola.

The Short-Lived Electric Railway

On one of his trips east, I. B. Perrine was entertained by Thomas A. Edison in his New Jersey workshop where the "Wizard of Menlo Park" explained his new invention: a greatly improved storage battery. I. B. went there with the idea of building an interurban railway to connect the new towns he had helped to create, and he learned that Edison's battery would make such a railway possible without costly overhead wires.

[Edison] *promised that Twin Falls would have the first Edison storage-battery-operated cars west of New York City.*

—Arthur Hart, Idaho State Historical Society (1982)

Perrine's plan was for a railway that would connect Twin Falls to Kimberly and Buhl and include a scenic run to Shoshone Falls. On 23 May 1912 he purchased two motor-traction cars; the first car arrived on 29 April 1913. On 4 May, a test run gave prominent citizens and their guests a free ride to Buhl and back over the Oregon Short Line tracks. Two months later, the Cutter May and Company of Chicago bought $55,000 worth of bonds.

The original scenic route of the railway was to be a fifteen mile loop by way of the canyon rim to the Shoshone and the Twin Falls, then back on Kimberly Road. The project proved to be too costly, and the plan for the interurban connections was dropped in favor of having only one track to Shoshone Falls and back. In September 1913 the initial rails and electric lines were laid on the route to Shoshone Falls. A special Shoshone Falls excursion ride for the Twin Falls Railway Company's officers was arranged for 28 September 1914.

On 4 October, Opening Day, from four to five hundred people rode to Shoshone Falls. The route began on Sixth Avenue S between the Oregon Short Line passenger depot and Benoit's bottling plant (now Depot Grill). The tracks proceeded up Shoshone Street almost to Main Avenue, turned left behind the Perrine Hotel where more passengers boarded, then up Second Street N and behind the courthouse for passengers. On Sundays, at the Justamere Hotel across the street, passengers could enjoy a brunch served on china plates. The railway continued north over to Blue Lakes Boulevard

and finally, at Falls Avenue, the route turned east and went on to Shoshone Falls. The return trip was the same except that the tracks came down Shoshone Street all the way to the depot. Round trip fare was forty cents.

> *People made trips to view the falls and enjoy picnics in the shade of the huge juniper trees that lined the bank of the river.*
>
> —Anna Hansen Hayes

Ned R. McCracken leased the railway line on 31 August 1916 for one year with a three-year option to renew. Ned had plans to run a gas motor truck on the rails, but before the year was up, McCracken's company went on the block at a sheriff's sale. The offering price was $31,130.93. The Edison batteries went to Bowman's UCC Ranch in Nevada to be their sole source of electricity.

Perrine's electric train suffered the fate of the horse and buggy: Replaced by the automobile.

Chapter 7

A Unique First Decade

Twin Falls itself was unique in that the town was planned from the start. Other western settlements, like the mining towns that just "sprang up" in gulches of gold and the cowtowns that just "happened" at end-of-the-drive railroad terminals, have mere records of development; Twin Falls has a history.

Planning Brought Results

The Twin Falls Land and Water Company picked the location, purchased the land, and incorporated its Twin Falls Townsite Company to plan and manage the townsite until the town could become self-governing. The townsite's engineer-planners even got input from one of I. B. Perrine's houseguests, E. A. Masqueray, who was an eastern architect with experience in laying out a World's Fair site.

But as management went into its second year, this barren sagebrush town didn't have so much as running water or electricity. Who, besides the men invested in the irrigation project, would be crazy enough to buy land and live in this desolate desert town? Perrine's associates and Chicago-based promoters had to apply enormous amounts of money and influence to convince easterners and midwesterners to come to Twin Falls. And come they did, to inspect a promise for the future: "The greatest irrigation project in the U.S.A." with its supporting town.

In Chicago's Loop District, H. L. Hollister and Company occupied the second floor of a corner commercial building. There in its large windows, Harry L. Hollister exhibited displays of Idaho fruit, grains, and vegetables that attracted dryfarmers, suppliers, warehousemen, other businessmen and professional men. Signs on the building read:

IDAHO HOMES IN THE TWIN FALLS COUNTRY
FREE EXHIBIT OF IRRIGATED PRODUCTS

—The Perrine Family Archives

Chicagoan Mark Bennett produced glossy brochures with enticing photos and texts. He arranged accommodations at Twin Falls's new luxury hotel for trainloads of prospective buyers. They came to see for themselves the rich farmland and well-planned town shown in Bennett's brochures. Amidst the flurry of building and farming activity they saw the town rise and the land green up before their eyes. Meanwhile, Perrine's and Waters's gold-medal-winning "Irrigated Products" from "Twin Falls Country" were attracting attention at World's Fairs.

I.B. PERRINE EXHIBITING WHEAT

Land-seekers received postcards with amazing settlement photographs taken by Clarence Bisbee and distributed by Charles Diehl of the *Twin Falls News* . . .

> *to dispel rumors in the East that nothing would grow in western sagebrush country, that there were no schools, churches, or other signs of civilization on the forsaken desert land . . .*
>
> —Mary Ann Smith and Helen Swan, CSI students

With the completion of Milner Dam, contractors and laborers, freighters and shopkeepers moved to Twin Falls to build the town, the canal system, and the railroad. Many bought town lots, many others lived in Rock Creek Canyon.

> *The Far West attracted foreign nationals for the same reason it drew people from the States. . . . Although their roll is sometimes overlooked today, they were a vital element in the regional social structure and gave it much of its unique flavor.*
>
> —John W. Evans, author of *Powerful Rockey* (1990)

The New Settlers Set the Tone

Not only did Perrine's land promotion create a great demand for real estate, the demanders had the money. Townsite lots were first available for $400–$500. In less than a year, prices went up to $1,500–$2,500 per lot. The town was being settled largely by a prosperous class of people—"most of them well dressed"—who set the tone. One such settler Joseph H. Seaver, a representative of the Kuhn Brothers who built the Northside Canal System, helped many young men get started in business in Twin Falls.

Twin Falls settlers created those "signs of civilization" that Bisbee's postcards touted. They built a school, organized churches, and started civic organizations. They created and served on school, fair, health, and library boards. They were elected to local and state governments. And they boasted that their town had a school before it had a saloon.

> *There were five saloons in Twin Falls and it was not considered safe for a woman to walk past one of them unescorted.*
>
> —Twin Falls High School Student Publication, 1944

When gambling came into town with the saloons, it was protested, and the village trustees passed an ordinance in 1905 that prohibited gambling. The situation came to a head that summer as told by Trustee Sam T. Hamilton:

> *One evening officers raided the basement of this building* [the Headquarters Saloon] *and took into possession the gaming tables, cards, and all the furnishings and equipment. The next morning, under the direction of John E. Hayes and his lieutenants, several hayrack loads of sagebrush were hauled and piled in the intersection of Main and Second Street E* [in front of the Blue Front Café]. *All the gambling devices were then placed on the pile of sagebrush and burned.*

The Anti-Saloon League of Idaho called for a mass meeting in October, and another ordinance was passed that closed the saloons from 10 P.M. to 7 A.M.

In 1907 the new town was paid a visit by one of I. B. Perrine's old friends William Jennings Bryan. Bryan, who ran for president in 1895 and 1899, was campaigning for a third (unsuccessful) try. That year Twin Falls residents started the Idaho Free Traveling Library. Edith Barnes sold pots of beans at W. Zenas Smith's bakery to raise money, and the women held rummage sales. Anna Hayes drove a cart and pony belonging to Grace Seaver to pick up donations of books and magazines and used furniture. They rented and furnished a room over Bainbridge Grocery in the Harder Building on Main Avenue, and citizens took turns as librarian. The Idaho Free Traveling Library would move five times in the thirty-two years between its inception in 1907 and the 1939 opening of the Twin Falls Public Library on Second Street E.

The Social and Civic Whirls Began Immediately

The jolliest, most enthusiastic crowd of people you ever saw.

—Grace Seaver

While the Rock Creek community was enjoying square dances hosted by Lucy Stricker, Twin Falls ladies enjoyed blossomtime picnics at the Blue Lakes Ranch of Hortense Perrine. Also like Lucy, Hortense played the organ for many Twin Falls functions. The organ belonged to Blanche Ramsey whose husband Fred was the assistant marshal and a village trustee. And, Mrs. P. was a fund-raiser who urged contributions from guests at Blue Lakes and provided the largest subscription to the Baptist building fund for Twin Falls's first church.

Members of the Homeless Twenty social group formed the Twin Falls Commercial Club in July 1905 "to study the water situation." That fall, the typhoid outbreak called the town's first physicians to civic duty, and Doctors Clouchek, Boyd, and Pike created a Health Commission and a Board of Health. The Twin Falls Commercial Club would take on many civic projects that would lead to its reorganization as the Twin Falls Chamber of Commerce in 1920.

While the town's men started their many service organizations and fraternal orders—Masons, Odd Fellows, Elks, Kiwanis, et al—the women started their own service clubs; some were affiliated with statewide and nationwide institutions. Dr. Clouchek's wife Emma started the Syringa Club in 1906.

> *The Syringa Club was for women who longed for an opportunity to enrich their lives with music, drama, literature, and other fine arts.*
>
> —Lorayne O. Smith, *The Times-News* staff (1991)

The Syringa Club was federalized in 1907, and the next year its name was changed to the Twentieth Century Club. Dues were two dollars, and by 1911 this club had more than one hundred members. Primarily a philanthropic organization, the club provided a variety of social events as well. Through its six departments this club would tackle such issues as water pollution, care of the elderly, day care, alcohol and drug abuse, and illiteracy. The Twentieth Century Club's donations, some as large as fifteen hundred dollars, would benefit strictly Twin Falls projects such as those of the City Parks Department and the local Salvation Army.

A Bible study class, also started by Emma Clouchek, would become the Business and Professional Women's Club in 1916. Emma Clouchek would serve in the Idaho State House of Representatives in 1931–1932 and then would be elected National Committee Woman for the Idaho Republican Party to serve for fourteen years.

Entertainment Had a Jolly Tone

Twin Falls settlers were eager for outdoor entertainment. James A. Waters's grove of locust trees on Falls Avenue at Locust Street attained a growth of from five to eight and a half feet in just five months, and as soon as shade appeared, picnickers from the whole community made it their gathering place. "The Locust Grove" became the site of the Old Settlers Annual Picnic. Waters was on the Twin Falls School Board for twelve years, and he would serve on the Twin Falls County Fair Board most of his life. In the Idaho legislature for two terms, 1917–1918 and 1921–1922, James A. Waters would introduce a bill to create an Idaho State Department of Agriculture.

Then there was the circus with its parade.

> *The Sells-Floto Circus came* [in 1907] *in a parade down Main Street in a foot of mud. Patrons took box lunches.*
>
> —Gus Kelker, *The Twin Falls Morning News* staff

FLOTO CIRCUS PARADE

> *For several years we got to watch the circus come to town via Addison Avenue. The circus had been unloaded at Minidoka and then traveled via hoof and a few motorized trucks to Twin Falls to perform. Most of the animals were inside boxed cages, but the elephants were very much in evidence pulling the wagons or walking in the caravan. We saw the brightly painted cages and calliope and caught glimpses of some of the other animals.* —Margaret D. Rude, CSI student

Killed by a tiger on 1 May 1907 was a baby girl. This story was told to Jewel L. Von Ins:

> *All eyes were glued on the main act—the tigers. A young tiger, not yet completely trained, failed to obey his trainer and darted out of the ring. He leaped several feet at a time, growing wilder every minute, then without warning he leaped at Mrs. Rozell, who was standing almost petrified with fright, holding her baby* [Ruth], *less than a year old. The tiger grabbed the baby by the throat, severing the jugular vein, then started to leap for the door, where many frightened people had headed. At that moment, Mr. Bell fired 5 shots at the tiger. The stunned and dying animal crawled out of the tent door and died.*
>
> —Jean Day, a 14-year-old boy

> *The tiger was tracked down in Rock Creek canyon and shot.*
>
> —Kelker's version per Wanda Hoag, nine years old at the circus

Several injuries were reported in July 1909 when horses were frightened by wild animals.

Twin Falls had other big tent attractions. The Taylor Players first had a tent on the corner of Second Avenue and Second Street N before performing in a theater. Evangelist Mattie Crawford came to Twin Falls and set up her big tent with its sawdust aisles ("sinners hit the sawdust trail") at Main Avenue and Third Street E. She was described as looking more like a movie star than a preacher in her white satin gowns. For many years the Chautauqua raised its big canvas tent in City Park and would fold it permanently in the depression.

E. A. Olden was hired in 1907 as the city's first paid park superintendent at seventy-five dollars per month. Every Fourth of July Olden had the wonderfully musical Flynn Merry-go-round put up in City Park. A wooden bandstand was built in 1910 for the City Band. This charming—but acoustically erratic—bandstand would be succeeded in 1935 by the big, lava rock band shell.

BAND STAND

There were sports and sportsmen. The Comets baseball team was sponsored by the Twin Falls Athletic Association and managed by J. E. White who was in real estate and insurance. In 1908 the Twin Falls Athletic Park was built in Bickel Field with a grandstand that seated five hundred, bleachers, and benches along the sidelines. Businesses customarily closed shop on afternoons of the ball games so owners and employees alike could attend the games. Charles Krengel was chosen the team's captain in 1910.

A big exhibition game on 9 November 1915 would draw a bigger crowd to Twin Falls than to any other town on tour including Salt Lake City. The American League Allstars team would battle the National League team to a 4–4 tie. "Cold weather prevents fast play, many errors," the newspaper would report. Then World War I would suspend "The Game," and Twin Falls would have to wait until 1939 to get another team.

> *The first game* [hunting] *law was written in 1864 after Idaho became a Territory and it closed big game hunting between February and July.* —Carl Nellis, Idaho Fish and Game Department (2001)

Idaho license fees—combination fish and game—were first established in 1903: resident males, one dollar; non-residents, five dollars; women, children, and Civil War veterans, free. Regulations made in 1911 limited the fish catch to the number of pounds per species.

Jeweler Walter Priebe was joined by Lud Drexler and Bill Malberg in 1910 to form the first sportsmen's club. They called it the Southern Idaho Fish and Game Association, and Lud would be the club's secretary for thirty-one years. In 1915 the Association would bring fifteen Chinese pheasants to Twin Falls and Priebe would make pens and breed them. By 1918 when the Chinese pheasant would become a game bird, Priebe would be producing up to three hundred birds a year. The Riley sisters Etta and Stella would pay $5 for rooster skins and $3 for hen skins at their millinery shop.

> *Around 1934 there was a bounty on magpies and their eggs. Priebe paid two cents a head and a penny for each egg that me and my brother turned in. We made from fifteen cents to twenty-five cents and considered this well worth our time.* —Don Dean (2003)

Walter Priebe would be invited to Washington, D.C., as one of two delegates from Idaho to help in founding the National Wildlife Federation in 1936. From this would come the Idaho Wildlife Federation. Priebe's Southern Idaho Fish and Game Association would be renamed the Twin Falls Wildlife Federation.

There were theaters and other entertainment. Admission was ten cents to the Benoits' theaters, which were the town's firsts. Built in 1909 the Iris was at 325 Shoshone Street S and the Dime was at 130 Main Avenue S. Both showed silent moving pictures that movie-goers called "the flickers."

> *Men would get off the train at the depot with hardly any money. But for ten cents they could spend all night in the theater—and sleep there.*
>
> —Robert Benoit

The first Orpheum Theater opened the following year at 129 Shoshone N. Then came the Isis next door and the Lyric across the street. Tommy Lloyd's Ice Cream Parlor with its fancy wire chairs and penny candy was a favorite stop after the flickers.

Roller skating rinks were popular and the town had several. Before the town had dance halls, the old Dewey Hotel at Shoshone Falls was the place for public dances. The Dewey was closed in 1910, so the Elks Club in the McCornick Building was chartered that year for a dance to the music of the "Twin Falls Band and Orchestra." In 1912 the Twentieth Century Club and the Apollo Club presented Gilbert and Sullivan's *The Mikado* at the Lyric Theater.

> *The most perfect club party ever given in Twin Falls was enjoyed by the Bachelor Boys and their friends at the Masonic Hall.*
>
> —*The Twin Falls News*, 26 December 1913

A unique community with lively, competent, and confident people saw nothing but good times ahead at the close of Twin Falls's first decade.

Chapter 8

World War I and Post–War Years, 1914–1921

A World War (WWI) Helped Agriculture

The war that erupted in Europe in 1914 touched off a four-year boom in this country. The irrigated acreage of the Twin Falls Tract expanded rapidly to produce potatoes, sugar beets, clover seed, beans, and orchard crops. Twin Falls County led the state in the average production per acre of alfalfa, hay, wheat, oats, barley, and corn.

> *Father worked eighty acres and was proud of his straight furrows, weedless fields, and high production. A 20- to 25-man crew gathered to run all harvest machines and horses and wagons. Women gathered at each farm to make the noon meal.* —Margaret D. Rude

At the Twin Falls Land and Water Company's experimental farm, scientists proved that the soil and climate of Twin Falls County was well adapted to sugar beets. But without a sugar factory in the area, sugar beets were recommended for livestock feed. In 1915 the Amalgamated Sugar Company of Ogden, Utah, built its Twin Falls factory two miles southeast of town at a newly constructed railroad spur. The company then contracted with thirty-three local farmers to grow sugar beets on five thousand acres, and in the fall of 1916 the factory began producing White Satin Sugar. The following year, the Utah Construction Company (UCC, owner of the Shoesole ranches) built feed lots at the sugar factory where local cattle were fed the sugar waste, molasses. Beginning in 1920 the cattle were trailed from the feed lots to the slaughterhouse at the Independent Meat Company.

In 1916 Twin Falls County got a fairground. Few fairs were held after that first one in Twin Falls in 1905. A school exhibition was held at the Washington School west of Filer in 1912. The next year, another school exhibition was held at Union School east of Filer near Curry Crossing. In 1915 Filer businessmen advertised the first "great fair" to be held in the county with orations, exhibits, races of all kinds, as well as a tug-o-war and a greased pig to catch. After consumption of all the lemonade and ice cream that everyone could consume, the festivities would be topped off with horse races and harness races. Filer citizens knew a good thing when they saw it:

> *The local committee selected the site east of Filer where originally many horse races were held. The Idaho Store Company, Ltd. . . offered the 40-acre site for $250 an acre. . . . The full amount* [$10,000] *was raised, in cash, in exactly five days! . . . The citizens of Filer offered the land to the county with the stipulation that a county fair must be held every year. If the fair was discontinued, the land and buildings would revert to the original donors for division.*
>
> —Mary Ramseyer, CSI student

"Filer Field Day, 1916" became the Twin Falls County Fair. Exhibits by I. B. Perrine showed that he continued to diversify: his Blue Lakes Nursery Orchard and Ranch was listed as Breeders of Thorobred Shropshire Sheep.

Twin Falls Joined in the War Effort

Women rolled bandages for the Red Cross and practiced shooting until they could "hit the Kaiser at long or short range." Several rural women's clubs banded together in 1915 to form the Rural Federation of Twin Falls County. They turned a 25-by-32-foot brick building at 151 Second Avenue N (now a parking lot) into a shelter "to assure both privacy and comfort for the many women who visit this city on shopping trips." As the war in Europe wore on, their Ladies' Rest Room was turned into a refugee work room. A children's group performed *The Queen of Hearts* to raise money for the emergency relief fund. In 1917 Charlie Walgamott returned to Twin

Falls from Montana and began to write his entertaining serial stories "Six Decades Back" for the *News*.

America entered World War I to end it. On 18 June 1916, Company D was formed in Boise from the Idaho National Guard for a Mexican Border Expedition. The newly married Charles Krengel, whom we last saw in 1912 inventing things in his blacksmith shop, was called to active duty "to fight Pancho Villa." The company trained in Arizona, returned to Boise, and was mustered out on 27 January 1917. On 26 March 1917 America entered World War I, a war in which horses and mules moved guns, supplies, and armies. Company D was again mobilized in Boise. Sent to France for eighteen months were Capt. Charles "Cap" Krengel and Harry Benoit, among others.

> *During WWI, the tracks of the short-lived 1912–1913 spur of the Idaho Southern Railroad between Oakley and Milner were taken up and sold for iron.* —Bessie Wright, historian (1990)

> *To keep the spirits up, the city hired a bandmaster.*
> —Fred Sanger, musician (1999)

In 1918 morale was low. Canadian-born J. T. Bainbridge, a former bugler with the Royal Canadian Mounted Police, was hired as bandmaster. Bainbridge, who would become the high school music teacher, held special City Band concerts in City Park that summer to boost morale. Several area residents also performed with the Second Idaho Regimental Band:

> *. . . the best and most thoroughly equipped musical organization in the inter-mountain country.* —*The Twin Falls Morning News*

In March 1918, when the U.S.A. was one year into the war, Mayor F. F. Bracken proclaimed that growing sugar beets was a "patriotic duty." The Twin Falls County Commission set a quota of ten thousand acres to meet the country's apparent need for sugar. The Twin Falls Council of Defense gave all idle men a choice: "Go to work on the farms at modest pay or leave the community." But the war ended in November and the market for sugar declined. Returning veterans found the fields they tramped and hunted before the war irrigated and off limits to them.

The Armistice was signed at 11 A.M. on 11 November 1918. The next year, Harry Benoit returned home to practice law.

> [Cap Krengel returned to his shop and] *began manufacturing sagebrush grubbers and alfalfa crowners, just two of his seventy-six patented inventions. These machines were marketed in seven western states, Canada, and Mexico. Krengel trailer hitches are sold in all fifty states.*
> —Jean Cilek and Matt Thomas (1990)

Two amendments to the U.S. Constitution followed World War I in rapid succession. The 18th Amendment was ratified in 1919 and ushered in fourteen years of Prohibition. In 1920 the 19th Amendment gave women the right to vote.

Wartime Prosperity Meant Construction

A flurry of construction in Twin Falls during the World War I years produced some of the finest buildings extant. Brick replaced lumber in construction; by 1916 the number of lumber companies had dropped from seven to four. That year saw the Twin Falls Building and Loan Association open an office in the Perrine Hotel.

The boom year was 1917. Twin Falls got a neoclassical-style U.S. Post Office Building at Main Avenue and Second Street W (since 1961, the School Administration Building) and the handsome Herriott Building on Second Street at Second Avenue W. The elegant Twin Falls Title and Abstract Company Building at 202 Shoshone Street E (recently the Magic Valley Bank) was built in the Renaissance revival style of architecture in terra cotta, as was the new Orpheum Theater in 1921.

The new Lavering Theater and Furniture Store with its lovely high double-arched face on Second Avenue at Second Street E (now Blacker Furniture) boasted the first electric sign in 1917 by Cosgriff Sign Company. Also that year the Twin Falls Bank and Trust Building (Wells Fargo Bank today) got its street clock which became so much a part of the streetscape that one city council excluded it from compliance with a sign ordinance. (This clock does not give the temperature, but it continues faithfully to tell the time.)

Built in 1918 at 130 Shoshone Street E the Idaho Theater seated 538, had the only theater pipe organ in town and held weekly wrestling matches. Across the street at 129 Shoshone Street N the vacated Orpheum Theater would be remodeled and renamed the Rialto Theater in 1922, and the Idaho would move to Main Street N.

The churches that would surround the city park area were begun in this construction period. In 1917 the neoclassical Presbyterian Church on Fifth Avenue at Second Street N was built designed by John Visser, architect for the Justamere Hotel in the same block. The Methodist Church was completed with an addition to the 1909 Gothic chapel. In 1920 St. Edward's Catholic Church was built in the Renaissance revival style. Later, in 1929, would be the construction of the classical First Christian Church.

Shoshone Street acquired two large apartment buildings contracted by William C. Reed, brickwork by Bobier: Rex Arms at 312 Shoshone E in 1918 and Reed Apartments at 833 Shoshone N in 1920. The expansion that year of the Twin Falls Bank and Trust Company along Main Avenue S took out the building that had housed Koto's Café for twelve years. Tom Koto had Reed build his "Koto Building 1920" on Main Avenue N. Next to this the new Orpheum Theater was built in 1921 by the Twin Falls Amusement Company, or "TFA Inc. 1920" as seen on the façade.

In 1920 the BPOE moved from the second floor of the McCornick Building to its impressive new Elks Lodge on Shoshone Street at Second Avenue N. The Addison T. Smith Building (recently Abbott's Garage) went up at 303 Shoshone Street S. This building and Addison Avenue were named for the Idaho congressman who served Twin Falls from 1913 to 1933.

ELKS LODGE

The Twin Falls County Commission established a Twin Falls County Hospital Board in 1917 to build a 36-bed hospital west of the city limits. Dr. T. O. Boyd sued the county to stop construction and to buy, instead, his hospital on Third Avenue W that was three blocks from the Cottage Inn (the recent site of Koppel's Browzeville) then being leased to the board for the care of indigents. The doctor lost, and construction continued with W. C. Reed the contractor; the cost, just over $60,000. On 29 June 1918 the Cottage patients were transferred to the new facility and the County Hospital was opened to the public. Suddenly, the Spanish flu epidemic—which took twenty-two million lives worldwide; 525,000 in the United States—hit Twin Falls. The new hospital was forced to open an annex to care for the flu victims. Of 117 admitted, fourteen died. Schools were closed for several weeks.

Several private 10- to 25-bed hospitals and a clinical laboratory could not compete with the county-supported hospital. Dr. John Morgan who had operated his Physicians and Surgeons Hospital for ten years transferred his patients and equipment to the County Hospital and folded. Boyd Hospital was sold in 1920 to Catholic sisters and was renamed La Merced Hospital, but finances forced the hospital's return to Dr. Boyd who then sold it to three partners. Even under new management this private hospital could not compete with the public hospital. The shuffled Boyd Hospital would be converted in 1922 into the Park Hotel, "in a park setting."

Construction produced the 1919 Hansen Bridge—"the highest suspension bridge in America, if not the world"—and the 1920 Singing Bridge over Rock Creek. (This bridge was declared unsafe and condemned in 1995. When all else failed to demolish this seventy-five-year-old span, it was dynamited. In its place is the Old Towne Bridge.)

After a 1916 bond election, in which Twin Falls residents approved of $80,000 for a waterworks system, the City Council passed an ordinance to create a Waterworks Department. In a 1918 bond election, another $37,500 was approved to expand the water system. The Fire Department replaced its 1908 steam fire engine with a 1921 American-LaFrance Triple Combination Pump Engine and Hose Motor Car for $20,000.

School Programs Progressed

The Parents and Teachers Association (PTA) was organized in 1915. The PTA mothers started the first hot lunch program in 1921 that supplied a cup of hot soup for each child that walked more than seven blocks from home bringing a bag lunch; the pupils that lived closer went home for lunch. Anna Hansen (Mrs. John E.) Hayes would be an officer for many years, including president of the Idaho State PTA. From 1949 to 1952, Mrs. Hayes would serve as president of the National PTA.

Bickel School was outgrown by 1915 but would continue to be used until replaced in 1938. Washington School at North Five Points (Rite-Aid location) opened in 1916, the last year that left-handed children were required to change to using their right hand. One Halloween the Washington School kids took up the wooden sidewalk planks from downtown and laid them end-to-end down Shoshone Street to make a sidewalk to their school so they didn't have to walk in the mud.

> *Washington Elementary School had a first in Idaho history. On June 14, 1919, teacher Juanita Dean was given a year's leave of absence. When school opened in September, she returned and she was the only female teacher in the state of Idaho who admitted to being married! She had to be hired on a day-to-day basis and a lot of noses went high in the air all over the state of Idaho at the awful thing Washington School in Twin Falls was doing. A married female teacher!! Completely unheard of!! Absolutely uncouth!!* —Evelyn Foster, CSI student

The Twin Falls Chapter of the Daughters of the American Revolution (DAR) was organized in March 1917 with the purpose of preserving America's patriotic history. Its programs would come to include the American History Essay Contests for junior high school students, Good Citizen Awards for high school students, and nursing scholarships.

New and Old Businesses Prospered After the War

Standard Printing went on line in 1917. In 1919 the Burkholder Furniture Store opened in the 1909 Johnson Building on Second Avenue W at Shoshone Street, and Claude Brown's Music Company opened at 143 Main E.

We met Jake Arrington in 1911 when he built housing for sheepherders and their valuable dogs. After working on the electric railway to Shoshone Falls, Jake helped build the sugar factory and the town's new water system, the Sande Building and the U.S. Post Office Building. In 1919 Jake and his brother Grover built a grocery store at 502 Main S (now Smazal's Business Techs) which was unique in having a notions counter. The Arringtons sold Jake's own Leghorn hens' eggs, bulk dried beans—use a scoop, bananas hanging from the ceiling by a rope, vinegar by the barrel—fill your own jug from the spigot, coal oil for lamps, crackers in a barrel, and bread—ten cents. Jake made deliveries by horse and buggy and also had a milk and ice cream wagon. He stopped by the high school at noon, rang a bell, and charged his student customers five cents for two cones and everyone else the same for one cone.

Drury Park and the Drury Park Grocery was a woman's work. A young Nebraska couple Charles and Frances Stephens arrived in dusty Twin Falls in 1906, settled down, and started their family with a son and a daughter. Frances, a talented pianist, was the town's first piano teacher. While Charles worked for the Twin Falls Canal Company, Frances dreamed of beautifying their westside corner of the Twin Falls sagescape with a park. With the help of her mother Getty Drury, who had joined the Stephenses, the neighborly Gillette family, and Mayor W. H. Eldridge, Frances collected enough money by 1917 to buy the triangular lot where Fourth Avenue and Sixth Street W met Washington Street. All the neighborhood kids plus Frances's own two pitched in to clear sagebrush and plant grass, flowers, and trees to make Drury Park (which today hosts the town's horseshoe pitching enthusiasts).

In 1921 Charles continued to work long hours checking canal banks and turning out water for the farmers; Frances went into business. Her first venture was a used clothing store, then came the Drury Park Grocery closer to home. Being very much a family business, the store would survive for many years until Frances's death in 1956 at age seventy-seven, three years after Charles's death at age eighty.

Sabala's boardinghouse was a Basque *posada.* During the first two decades of the twentieth century, many Basques came to Idaho on work contracts—usually as sheepherders and domestics—and settled mainly around Boise. They sent money home, and after about ten years, many returned to Spain to buy their own businesses. In 1920 Francisco and Florentina Sabala from Spain via Boise opened Twin Falls's first Basque boardinghouse at 214 Second Street S, in the vacated Cottage Inn with twelve bedrooms, two bathrooms and one bath tub. The Sabalas paid twenty-five dollars a month and charged a daily fee of one dollar for a room and three meals. Sheepherders spent their evenings in the card room playing a Basque card game of Mus; the women usually played Casino.

> *Business was good for the Sabalas during the winter months, but harder times came during the spring and summer seasons when boarders returned to their jobs of herding sheep.*
>
> —Debbie Mendiola Marshall (1990)

The Sabala family business would continue after Florentina's death in 1926 until 1942 when Francisco would die leaving eight children and one grandchild.

We met Harry Brizee in 1909 when he bought a sheet metal shop.

> *During the past few years, this firm has played an important part in the building of this city since a large number of prominent buildings have been installed with furnaces furnished by this company.*
>
> —*The Coyote*, Twin Falls High School's 1917 edition

Harry's brother Leland joined the firm in 1919 and they moved the shop to its present location at 227 Second Avenue E. Brizee Metal Works took on the Lennox Furnace Company line in 1921.

Between 1906 and 1910 we saw three men—Brose, Terrill, and Jungst—establish separate meat markets on Main Avenue, then merge to form the Independent Meat Company. Manager Jungst moved the abattoir from the bottom to the top of Rock Creek Canyon in 1919 and hired Otto Florence (Sr.). Next year began the trailing of local cattle from the feed lot at the sugar factory to the meat company's slaughterhouse. Here was the supply of beef for the company's retail outlets. Florence left Twin Falls in 1921 and would return with a wife and two small sons in 1925 to a new job as foreman of the packing plant.

Chapter 9

The Farm Depression, 1921–1929

Drought devastates crops. Canal companies curtail deliveries.

—1919 headlines

Tough Times Were Ahead

Many crops were lost to the severe water shortage that developed in 1919. The federal government looked for a new reservoir site and in 1921 filed on the American Falls location. By then agriculture prices collapsed and Idaho went into a farm depression that would last twenty years. Farm wages were so low that in 1923 the Amalgamated Sugar Company brought in workers from North Dakota and hired Mexicans to get in the beet harvest, all done by hand. The factory was forced to close several years: 1924, 1926, 1928, and 1934.

A potato farmer who lived just east of Twin Falls rose to the challenge of the farm depression. Joe Marshall worked with banks to save farms from foreclosure by supervising farm operations and advising farmers with their problems, such as the deterioration of the quality of Idaho potatoes. Joe Marshall found clean, disease-free seed in Montana and Oregon, established a potato seed industry, and convinced farmers to use his specially grown certified seed. Through the efforts of this one Twin Falls County man, Idaho Russets became the best quality potato in the nation and commanded premium prices.

Marshall brought his family from Ohio to the Twin Falls irrigation project in 1902. In July 1903 at Shoshone, Joe was twenty-eighth of the thirty farmers who filed claims on the first segregation of the Twin Falls Tract. In 1937

Marshall would help organize the Idaho Potato Commission, and in 1946 delegates from all forty-eight states would vote him "Potato King," a title that would retire with him. Joe Marshall would die in 1964 at age eighty-seven after being hit by a car in front of his home on State Highway 50.

> *He wore* [overalls] *proudly as the uniform of a man who had spent his life in agriculture and loved the Idaho potato.*
>
> —James W. Davis, author of *Aristocrat in Burlap*

In this farm depression, many fruit trees—in the orchards that were expanded during the war to cover ten thousand acres—were pulled up to make room for the better paying crops of wheat, alfalfa, clover seed, sugar beets, barley, corn, and beans. Orchards failed because labor was intensive and hard to get. Beans needed cultivating at the same time the fruit trees needed spraying, and without sophisticated sprays, fruit had to be sorted and the diseased fruit picked out by hand. All the summer's expenses of spraying, pruning, clearing for harvest, and of pickers and sorters had to be paid before an apple was sold. Transportation of fruit out of the valley was yet another problem, and the climate was not dependable. By 1954 there would be only five hundred acres in orchard, in the Snake River Canyon where the soil was deeper and richer and the fruit ripened ten days earlier.

In this hard time, the dairy industry increased rapidly since the cost of feed was 30 to 50 percent lower in depressed southern Idaho. In 1922 the state reported more than eight thousand dairy cows in Twin Falls County; eight dairies were situated within two miles of Twin Falls, three of them less than a mile from town. Three more nearby ranches raised beef cattle, hogs, and sheep. (All this acreage is within Twin Falls city limits today.)

Pennies Were Pinched, Costs Were Contained

The Roaring Twenties did not roar a lot in Twin Falls. The *Twin Falls Morning News* reported humble times in simple terms on 5 July 1921:

> *The trip from Twin Falls to Boise on the Trask Bros. stage took 7½ hours. . . . Horlick's Malted Milk was delicious and safe for infants and invalids. . . . The American Tobacco Co. offered "111" cigarets at 15¢ a pack. . . . Babe Ruth had just hit home run #31 of the season. . . . Jack Dempsey was heavyweight champ again. . . . The paving of the road from Twin Falls to Kimberly would be done in two weeks. . . . Gasoline was 17¢ a gallon, butter eggs and fryers 25¢, potatoes 5¢ a pound, bread 10¢, bacon and T-bone steak 35¢.*

GAS PUMP

There were no comic strips, but jokes were reported.

Entertainment and recreation were free in the parks. Free summer band concerts in City Park continued under Jack Thorpe who was hired as Twin Falls second bandmaster in 1921.

> *Jack Thorpe was a short man, but when he conducted John Philip Sousa's* Stars and Stripes Forever, *he became ten feet tall—it was that exciting.*
>
> —Fred Sanger

Every Fourth of July the City Band played for street dances where corn meal was spread on the pavement, and fireworks were held on the courthouse lawn.

Harmon Park was acquired at this time. In 1924 William E. Harmon of New York had $100,000 to grant for city parks. The Harmon Foundation offered sites to fifty communities with a population of three thousand or more and with a growth of at least 30 percent since 1900. When a chosen town had the money on deposit to cover upkeep for the first year ($300), Harmon would transfer the property to the town. This was a personal gift from Mr. Harmon, and if all conditions were not met, the property would revert to him, his heirs, or assigns. Twin Falls was the twenty-fifth town selected to get $2,000 to purchase property in Harmon's name. On 23 April 1926 four acres were conveyed from William E. and Katherine F. Harmon to the city of Twin Falls and named Harmon Park.

> *Four acres in orchard, trees pulled, ground leveled, put up a rock that holds the Harmon plaque.* —T. L. Douglas (1963)

When Dierkes Lake at Shoshone Falls opened to the public the next year, the Shoshone Falls Power Plant provided free night lighting for viewing the magnificent falls. That was the last year of its magnificence, however, for in 1927 the American Falls Dam went into operation and the flow to Shoshone Falls was then much reduced.

> *We lived at 550 Fourth Avenue W in the '20s, and we went to sleep hearing the roar of Shoshone Falls before the American Falls Dam was built.* —Merle Stoddard (1999)

There was barnstorming:

> *It was estimated that* [Charles A.] *Lindbergh would be over Twin Falls sometime during the noon hour. It is expected that he will circle a time or two at low altitude over Twin Falls Park so that the famous plane* [*Spirit of St. Louis*] *will be plainly visible from that point.*
> —*The Twin Falls Morning News*, 4 September 1927

> *Lindy was late . . . Half an hour later the real Lindy came, circled the city . . . dropped the* [scroll] *greeting and then rose in the air and started away on his trip to the state capitol.*
> —*The Twin Falls Morning News*, 6 September 1927

(The scroll, dated and signed by Charles A. Lindbergh, is on display at the Twin Falls Airport.)

There were other freebies, like "Meet me at the I. D."

> *Stores were the meeting place. People would go evenings to shop and visit. The stores were built with benches up front for customers to sit and wait for their order and chat. The grocery list would be given to the clerk who would fill out the order while customers waited or visited with friends.* —Ethel Corak, homesteader

No doubt, the best free entertainment to come out of the farm depression—aside from the cost of the radio—was the broadcast of programs from Radio Station KGIQ that went on the air in 1928 from the Park Hotel. The KGIQ studio was in the old Boyd Hospital's operating room with its sloping floors and drain hole right in front of the announcers.

Theaters provided much entertainment for a small charge of admission. In 1921 A. R. Anderson, manager of the Twin Falls Amusement Company, moved the Orpheum Theater to 146 Main Avenue N. Featured in this sumptuous, spare-no-expense theater were indirect lighting on dimmers and seats for nine hundred. Balcony tickets were twenty-five cents; main floor, thirty cents for a matinee or evening of feature movie, newsreel, cartoons, vaudeville, and coming attractions. This new Orpheum had an 8-piece orchestra for major movies.

The Lavering Theater's large stage and orchestra pit had been built for live theater. For major silent movies, such as *Covered Wagon*, a 15-piece orchestra was brought in. One twelve-year-old schoolboy was so inspired by that sound that he decided right then he would some day play in a theater orchestra. In 1925 at age fifteen, Fred Sanger began playing trumpet in the Orpheum's orchestra—and would also play in the High School Band and City Band all through high school. Vaudeville, then in decline, was featured only on Wednesday nights with such artists as Eddy Peabody on banjo. Sanger played in a 5-piece group on vaudeville nights and occasionally with two other musicians for Sunday matinees for two dollars a performance.

In 1927 the Business and Professional Women's Club brought in John Philip Sousa and his concert band to give Twin Falls a treat at the Orpheum Theater. At intermission Sousa conducted the Twin Falls High School Band in playing his celebrated *Sesquicentennial* (1776–1926) *March*. Sousa shook trumpeter Fred Sanger's hand. The "canned music" that was taped on the edge of film in 1928 brought in the "talkies" and put musicians out of business; Sanger left for the university at Moscow.

A big celebration was held at the new Twin Falls-Jerome Intercounty Bridge. Citizens of the two towns cheered as Hortense Perrine christened the structure with a bottle of sweet cider. Jerome celebrated with a barbecue and a Jerome-Burley football game; Twin Falls, with fireworks.

The Twin Falls-Jerome Intercounty Bridge was then termed the highest bridge of its type in the United States. —Gus Kelker

This toll bridge opened in October 1927, was 502 feet above streambed, and cost $650,000. I. B. Perrine's bridge at Blue Lakes was no longer necessary, so his Blue Lakes Road was rerouted to the new bridge. The toll was sixty cents per car and driver and five cents for each additional person.

> *The Snake River became a dumping ground for unwanted debris. When the Jerome-Twin Falls Bridge was completed, revelers brought their unwanted farm equipment—tractors, combines, etc.—to roll to the edge of the canyon, put them in gear and send them over in flames. . . . A local distributor took leftover produce. Large ranchers loaded garbage on trucks, backed them to the canyon wall, and dumped refuse. The practice ended only after an overly confident employee backed too far, and driver, truck, and garbage tumbled to destruction together.* —Larry Quinn, historian

Government and Businesses Struggled, Adjusted, or Expanded

Twin Falls voters chose a commission form of city government in 1922 with five commissioners, one of them the mayor, which would last until

1949. Twin Falls boasted of fifteen miles of paved streets, seventy-five miles of concrete sidewalks, and fifty-five miles of city pipelines. In 1926 the city got its first red traffic light, at Main and Shoshone.

But the construction boom that gathered momentum during World War I and carried over into the farm depression years eventually slowed to a halt. With the exception of the Orpheum, the Intercounty Bridge, and the First Christian Church, very little notable construction took place. One other exception was the American Legion Memorial Hall with a capacity of fifteen hundred people that was built in 1928 on Third Avenue at Second Street E (since 1998, home of South Central Head Start). This building ushered in the new Art Deco-style of architecture with patterned brick-work and a round-roofed face.

Any new businesses had to occupy existing buildings. The Babbels moved to Twin Falls in 1921 and opened a tailoring shop in the 1910 Booth Building (where Crowley's is today). Before that, Frederick W. Babbel moved his family from Salt Lake City to Buhl in 1919 and opened a general store. Babbel generously extended credit to the local farmers, and when the farm depression hit, Babbel found he could not collect, and his business folded.

> *It didn't help matters that my father always treated everybody to free ice cream every time the local baseball team won a game.*
>
> —Roy Babbel (1990)

With his new business in Twin Falls, Babbel was able to get all his bills paid in a few years. Before alterations were done on many of the garments that came in for tailoring, they needed dry cleaning, which was done by Doss Cleaners. That was when Babbel became interested in going into the dry cleaning business himself.

David Detweiler made a loan of five hundred dollars to an acquaintance in 1921 to start a coal yard at 138 Fourth Avenue S near the railroad. After a few months, David purchased the business for another thousand dollars and began the Detweiler Coal Company.

> *The original equipment consisted of one Model T truck, a team of plodding mules, and a delivery wagon.*
>
> —George C. Detweiler, son (1990)

Sales of about thirty thousand dollars were realized that first year. But the coal business was seasonal with the slack summer months eating up winter's profits. The solution for providing year around work was the automatic furnace, and in 1928 Detweiler brought to Twin Falls the Iron Fireman Automatic Stoker.

Krengel's Hardware was a sign of the times. Two events in 1926 proved that the automobile had indeed replaced the horse: (1) the centralized school system replaced its twenty-six horse-drawn busses with motor busses, and (2) Krengel's Hardware and Machine Shop closed out its blacksmith shop and expanded its hardware department with household fixtures, dishes, and lamps.

We left Clarence Allen in 1913, newly married, with an Optometry Salon in the balcony of Priebe's Jewelry Store and in watch-making, jewelry repair, and hand engraving. In 1926 he and his brother-in-law Fred B. Carson purchased Priebe's Jewelry Store, which they renamed Sterling Jewelry.

Historical Update: The year before he sold his store, Walter R. Priebe—outdoorsman, conservationist, bird bander and breeder—started the Rock Creek Fish Hatchery to stock the local lakes and streams for sport fishermen. Priebe persuaded the Southern Idaho Fish and Game Association, which he started in 1910, to buy the property in Rock Creek

Canyon and build the hatchery. This Association, which was renamed the Twin Falls Wildlife Federation, is the present owner of the hatchery. From 1938 to 1977, the State Fish and Game Commission leased the facility. Since then, the hatchery has been managed by the College of Southern Idaho Aquiculture Department to train students in commercial, not sport, fishery. The Walter R. Priebe Fish Hatchery was dedicated in 1991.

In 1924 Mrs. Ella M. White, an employee of Glenn Blue, purchased his Blue and Company Mortuary located in the store front of a building on Shoshone Street. Mrs. White changed the name to White Mortuary in 1928.

> *In 1925 the average cost of a funeral service in Twin Falls was $261, and the most common cause of death was pneumonia or heart trouble. Many young people in the 1920s and 1930s died of pneumonia.* [Mortuaries ran the ambulances and] *few ambulance bills exceeded $5.*
>
> —Jerry D. Holman (1990)

Also in 1928 an infectious meningitis epidemic hit the area taking twenty lives in two weeks. Schools closed as the city was quarantined, and the first cooperative Twin Falls County Public Health unit was formed. This unit consisted of three public health nurses who were paid $150 per month and a sanitary inspector who was paid $125 per month; their travel budget was $160. These expenses were funded by Twin Falls County, U.S. Public Health Services, and the Rockefeller Foundation.

The Sense of Community Was Changing

With many men seeking work and family housing through the 1920s, the population of Twin Falls increased by 30 percent to 10,821. Under Mayor R. E. Bobier a Zoning Committee was appointed in 1927 to plan for the growth of the city of Twin Falls, already well beyond its townsite. By the end of the decade and halfway into the farm depression, farm machinery had replaced the horse. The combine, which could be pulled by one man on a tractor along the windrows, replaced the steam threshing machine. Farmers no longer gathered to help their neighbors get in a harvest; farm women no longer pooled their dishes to serve the meals they once prepared for twenty-four men.

> *So many changes. I first noticed it in the late '20s when there were no more horses in the fields. And the disappearance of the steam threshing machine—that began the elimination of community effort.*
>
> —Edith Robertson, Twin Falls native (1999)

Spreading throughout rural southcentral Idaho was this sense of loss of community. And struggling with its increasing population and stagnating economy was Twin Falls, a shaky support for its troubled agricultural community.

TRACTOR AND BINDER

Chapter 10

The Great Depression, 1929–1935

The stock market crashed on 24 October 1929 setting off "the depression" that brought suffering over the next five years. Two local banks failed: the Twin Falls National Bank in November 1931 and Perrine's First National Bank of Twin Falls the next month. Only the Twin Falls Bank and Trust survived "The Crash."

Fruit prices went so low that fruit trees were cut up for firewood.

—Dr. Jim Gentry, CSI historian (2003)

Farmers Suffered More than Failed Banks

What depression? We were always poor.

—Jim and Ann Kimball, farmers (2002)

Twin Falls farmers were already ten years into a farm depression that would deepen for five more years. Idaho was in the midst of the ten driest years in its history. Local farmers, most of them originally dryfarmers from back east with no previous experience with irrigation, which was seriously curtailed, saw their incomes drop to less than half. Many left their farms, which fell to ruin and sagebrush.

Southern Idaho had 3.9 inches of rain in the 1933–34 year, and the sugar factory closed for the fourth time. Sugar beet crops were hit by a disease called "curly top," caused by a virus transmitted by the beet leafhopper. The USDA (Department of Agriculture) set up an entomology research laboratory at the corner of Blue Lakes Boulevard and Falls Avenue (Hasting's location). By 1938 the government scientists would have developed a resistant strain of beets. However, sugar content would never again reach the 1929 record of 18.59 percent. The bean crop was hit by the virus in 1924, and with bean varieties slower to develop, the disease would last until 1957. Harvesting by then would be almost one hundred percent mechanized.

Twin Falls Businesses Suffered

The effect of the failed economy on the city's pioneer businesses was a story of contrasts. While some went under, others thrived. Many changed hands. Most continued to provide the community with goods and services eking out a subsistence with the kind of imagination, grit, and perseverance that author Wallace Stegner honored with the title of "Stickers." Such was Harry Eaton who came to Twin Falls from Maine in the early 1900s. In 1917 he started his banking career as a teller and bookkeeper at the Twin Falls Bank and Trust; the bank and Harry Eaton became Stickers.

Some of our old friends couldn't stick it out. C. O. Meigs Implement Company, which was geared to the horse since 1905, found the horse replaced by the iron-wheeled tractor; Meigs's business folded. William Warberg sold his interest in the Warberg Coal Transfer and Storage Company to his partner in 1930 and retired to his farm. Koto's Café closed and Twin Falls lost "a special place to eat out." Tom Koto took his family to Jerome to help a brother with his café. After Tom's death in 1935, his widow and sons Tom and Ernest moved to Shoshone and opened a restaurant there; years later they would return to Twin Falls. Jake Arrington, landlord, concessionaire, construction worker, storekeeper, sold his horse-drawn ice cream wagon to Roy Babbel, burned all his customers' bills, and closed his grocery store with the notions counter. Jake would continue to live in Twin Falls to the age of 105 in 1993.

The construction business continued to suffer. Only one new building went up in Twin Falls during the depression: the Art Deco-style Burkholder's Furniture Store in 1931 on Shoshone at Second Avenue E (since demolished). Also built that year was the 9-hole Twin Falls Country Club with sand greens (now the Twin Falls Municipal Golf Course).

Stickers and How They Stuck

We had very little money . . . I remember when we had to "hock" most of our possessions to pay our bills, then buy them back, only to hock them again.
—Roy Babbel

While helping his father in the Babbel's Tailoring business, Roy Babbel also worked in an apple warehouse ten hours a day, six days a week, for fifteen cents an hour. If any man complained, he was told "There's the door"; others were ready to take his job. Roy also worked in I. B. Perrine's fruit orchard and drove a grocery delivery truck, often getting stuck in the muddy roads. Summers he ran his newly-acquired ice cream wagon making $2.50 on a good day, which was usually band concert day in City Park.

Clarence Allen, who purchased Walter Priebe's jewelry store in 1926 and renamed it Sterling Jewelry, was licensed by the U.S. government to purchase raw gold from miners who worked the Snake River during the depression. He processed the gold and shipped it to the assay office in Seattle.

The small but welcome margin helped the store considerably.
—Howard L. Allen (1990)

Historical Update: A couple of those placer miners were working along the river about two miles below Milner Dam. There they found an old bundle wedged in the rocks which contained the remains of a very old musket, axe, and beaver traps. The make of the gun proved to be from the time of Wilson Price Hunt's 1811 expedition, and it is believed that the bundle was lost there in his Cauldron Linn disaster. These artifacts are on display at the Idaho State Historical Museum in Boise.

Harry and Leland Brizee survived the depression years in their metal works by taking on innovative projects such as supplying the railroad with handmade metal stoves that kept East Coast-bound potatoes from freezing.

A. M. Sande added kindling sales to his Twin Falls Feed and Ice Company business. On a hunting trip to Twin Falls, Bing Crosby asked Mr. Sande to freeze and ship home his four pheasants. Bing was so pleased, he tipped Sande one dollar—almost a day's wages in the depression.

Some of the people who worked 10-hour days, six days a week, were paid fourteen to eighteen dollars every other week.

> *The men* [at Cosgriff's Sign Company] *would work every other day so everyone could have some income.* —Tom W. Moore (1990)

Cosgriff's was one of the oldest sign companies in Idaho with a Twin Falls shop at 228 Second Avenue W since 1906. Tom Moore, who would start his own sign company in the 1960s, would retain the Cosgriff's safe that kept their two most prized possessions: twenty-four-carat gold leaf and bootleg whiskey. Lee Logan who did the gold leaf lettering (today a lost art) would become one of Idaho's most beloved landscape artists.

Hamburger sold for five cents a pound, milk for ten cents a quart, and bread for six cents a loaf. After coming to Twin Falls from Kansas in 1930, H. O. "Fat" Higgins opened a restaurant at 235 Shoshone Street S that did not have a name and was known as Fat's.

> *HAMBURGERS 5¢ Buy 'em by the Sack.*
> *Chili 10¢ Beef Stew 15¢* —Lettering on Fat's windows

E. E. White, the "Maytag Man," came from Nevada in 1935 to open a branch of Wilson-Bates Appliance Company, which he then bought. White made many deals with down payments of poultry, cows, fruit or whatever a person had for trade.

David Detweiler, who had recently brought the Iron Fireman Automatic Stoker to Twin Falls, sold the Detweiler Coal Company to his sons Harry, George, and Claude. They changed the company name to Detweiler Brothers and entered the field of electrical appliances and refrigeration in 1933. The brothers would make the first installations of air conditioners in Twin Falls and sell their coal company to the Nye Brothers.

> *Grandma was furious when Grandpa* [John Nye] *brought home a chicken instead of cash.* —Pam Burgess Maughan (2001)

Al and John Nye, who established the Nye Brothers City Fuel Company in 1916 at Shoshone S and Maxwell by the railroad tracks, extended credit to many families for long periods of time. Sometimes they traded for a chicken or a sack of potatoes.

Otto Florence Sr. was foreman of the packing plant at the Independent Meat Company since returning from California in 1925 with a wife and two small sons.

> *Many early residents of Twin Falls remember as kids stopping at Independent Meat Market (the one located between the Orpheum and Roxy Theaters) to buy a five-cent pickle on their way to the movies.*
>
> —Mary Alice and Otto Florence Jr. (1990)

In the 1930s the company closed several of its downtown meat markets where its Falls Brand meats—and pickles—were sold. Under a government program, cattle came by rail from Nebraska and were slaughtered at Independent's slaughterhouse. In the depth of the depression, Otto Sr. was able to purchase one-third interest in the company.

> *. . . I was a boy, helping to trail cattle from the Amalgamated Sugar Company siding to the plant . . .* —Otto Florence Jr.

Hotels stuck through the depression.

> *The Perrine Hotel was the Crossroads. Any day you could see everybody in the county—they all came in to use the restroom.*
>
> —Fred Sanger

Fred Sanger—boy trumpeter in the Orpheum pit, High School Band, and City Band—had his college education interrupted "by poverty" for two years. Fred returned to Twin Falls and clerked at the Perrine Hotel, which then had a lobby after the court yard was roofed over. The lobby was the "unofficial headquarters" for the livestock industry where cattle- and sheepmen met with buyers. Also, for two or three months every fall, the lobby was HQ for the thirty potato brokers (today there is one) who placed orders for out-of-town buyers for carloads of potatoes to be shipped east. In 1930 ownership of the Perrine Hotel went from George Sprague to his brother-in-law

Thomas Robertson, and his son Richard Robertson would manage the hotel for more than thirty years. Richard's brother John became proprietor of the family's Irrigated Lands Company.

The Rogerson Hotel changed hands in 1933, and the new owners, the Hoops family, closed the hotel dining room. The next year Jenny Hoops Stewart opened the Rogerson Restaurant. The hotel would be remodeled in 1938 with something novel for that day: air conditioning in all the guest rooms.

Teenagers Pitched In

Youngsters lacked spending money during the depression, but they coped.

> *Saturday night was movie night. My date had one dollar and gave me the choice: We could buy gas or we could eat. We ate—and we walked. Everybody walked! People have forgotten that.*
>
> —Edith Robertson

After a movie or a high school dance, the place to go for cokes and ice cream was Wray's 24-hour Café in the Perrine Hotel or Pixton's Confectionery next to the Roxy Theater. When church groups did not approve of dancing in schools, students formed clubs and held dances in homes with Victrola music and refreshments. The Lavering was converted into Danceland where youngsters paid ten cents to dance to music by good local bands while parents danced to Big Bands two blocks away at the IOOF. Dances were also held in the Park Hotel's Radioland Ballroom owned by KGIQ which, in 1928, was one of the first radio stations to be licensed in the United States. In 1932 KGIQ was renamed KTFI and moved with its ballroom to the Herriott Building on Second Street W. Another form of entertainment for youngsters was watching KTFI radio broadcasts from behind the glass partition.

Teenagers hiked to Blue Lakes, which was "abandoned" in 1927, for hotdog roasts. Roller rinks were popular in the 1930s but would be converted to bowling alleys in the 1940s. Bicycles were cool, and boys, especially, enjoyed biking to Rock Creek to search for arrowheads and other Indian relics.

> *During the winter, the greatest playground was where the Centennial Mall is today. The Perrine Coulee overflowed as it froze, flooding the area, and we kids could ice skate and sled from where the Arctic*

Circle is now to the Turf Club. And in the summer there were gnarly old trees to climb, frogs, jackrabbits, snakes, everything a kid could want. We would bike to Dierke's Lake every day—it cost ten cents to get in—and the Snake River canyon was our playground from there to Pillar Falls. The only rule was to be home for dinner.

—Robert Benoit

Many teenagers worked for spending money or to help the family finances: Majestic Pharmacy paid them eighteen cents an hour; Penney's, nineteen cents; and the I. D., twenty-one cents. This was the first generation of girls to wear slacks and bobby sox—but not to school. Jake Arrington's daughter Velma worked in her dad's grocery store. One day gypsies visited the store and threatened that if she didn't give them cash from the register, they would steal groceries. Lucky for her, glass counters deterred them.

As one who was fortunate enough to have been a youngster in . . . those magical years of the '30s, I had a first hand seat . . . to see the arrival of the Gypsies . . . traveling as a clan in brightly colored wagons . . . pulled by a team of grey horses with beautiful harness with little silver tinkling bells . . . the vanguard of women on foot dressed in brightly colored loose fitting clothing. The problem was they snatched everything before them that wasn't bolted down!

—Ted Samples (1990)

Twin Falls youngsters saved the Twin Falls County Fair during the depression. A county fair had to be held every year to keep the land from reverting to the original owners, but in 1932 there was no money in the county treasury for a fair. So instead, a "4H & FFA County Fair" was held that year and for the next two years, until the county was again solvent.

On winter evenings, James A. Waters [County Fair Board member] *hitched up his sleigh and ran it to town from his farm and locust grove, picking up kids all around City Park and giving them rides with sleigh bells jingling.*

—Glenn Young (2000)

"New Pioneer" Businesses Got a Start

The Roxy was the world's largest theater, and Koehler had the town's largest heart.

We think you'll like our brand new theater. ROXY IS THE NAME! Because it was the name of our favorite cowpony and it also happens to be the name of the World's Largest Theater in New York City.

—Joe Koehler

Ernest R. "Joe" Koehler, a navy veteran of the Spanish-American War, managed the Idaho Theater from 1921 to 1930. When the talkies came in, Paramount Studios started buying up little theaters and Joe was fired. The next year, Joe opened the smaller but successful Roxy Theater at 130 Main Avenue N across from the Perrine Hotel. Admission was cheaper than the Orpheum up the block: adults, twenty-five cents; kids, ten cents. Joe was known for his big heart. He held a benefit matinee at his Roxy for the Ralph Brown family which had lost four children and their home in a fire. Tickets were "no less than fifty cents" with all proceeds going to the family. Joe's theater financed other ventures such as putting up many a jobless, hungry transient or family at a local boardinghouse with a breakfast to start the next day.

MAIN AVENUE N

Alfred O. "Snowball" Latham had a heart as big as Joe's. Snowball owned nine sports shops in Idaho. His Twin Falls store at 110 Main N was the gathering place for unemployed men. Snowball was another of Twin Falls's humanitarians in the 1930s who provided many a person in need with a meal, a room in a hotel, and clothes.

Snowball never turned a man away because he had no money in his pocket, but he would send a man "right out the door" if he heard the man's money could better be served by feeding his family.

—Mary Lee Aldrich Haug (1990)

In the shop's back room, men with time on their hands could shoot a game of pool or snooker or play a hand of poker or panginny. In the front of the shop was a counter with food and beverage, beer on tap (no liquor even after 1933), punchboards for the risk-takers, and places to just sit and talk with cronies. Any woman who came to the counter (women seldom ventured into such establishments in those days) was treated with courtesy as she ordered sandwiches and soft drinks "to go," and went. Snowball had a special concern for young people. After a game, the high school team and coach would be found at Snowball's counter being treated to hamburgers and milk shakes. Latham would die in 1939 leaving a wife and six children, one of them was Bob Latham.

Santa Bilbao's Basque boardinghouse was run by a remarkable woman. Basque women came to the United States to work in boardinghouses as cooks and housekeepers, and many settled in Boise. Santa Bilbao, newly divorced and with children, came from Boise to Twin Falls in 1930. In need of income she rented a seedy house on Main Avenue to run as a Spanish-Basque *posada*, and with her children's help, she put the building in shape for her business. Although Prohibition was in effect, Santa sold liquor to her boarders while the local police looked the other way, allowing the Basques their customs. The boarders gave no trouble on or beyond the premises.

Six years later, the house was suddenly sold and Santa had to move. Remarkably, in a time of depression this stranded lady got financing from a relative and built her own boardinghouse at 302 Second Avenue S. There she charged one dollar a day for a room and three meals, or thirty dollars a month. A French-Basque from California found the *posada* and rented a room off and on keeping all the room's keys, allowing no housekeeping. He did invite Santa into his room one day, and there was a little counterfeiting machine.

> *On his visits he was very generous. Well, needless to say, sometimes he paid with "new bills!" Santa had unknowingly taken them to the bank but no one ever was the wiser.*
>
> —Rosa Sofia, Isabel Mendiola, and Ruth Glenn (1990)

For twelve years the boarders at Santa Bilbao's Basque boardinghouse would celebrate holidays and hold dances with lively accordion music.

Twin Falls had another remarkable woman. In 1933, when Marian and Lambert "Bert" Langdon were on a shoestring, they bought a warehouse at 160 Fourth Avenue W to store hides, wool, pelts, and scrap iron and started a business called L. L. Langdon. At this time trout farm operators prepared their own feed, which included meat ground from unwanted cattle and horses; L. L. Langdon bought the hides, which would bring top prices during World War II. Bert would die at the end of that war in 1945. Marian Langdon would take over the business, raise her two children (one was Buzz Langdon) and three stepchildren, and be named Idaho State Mother of 1952, the youngest woman ever so honored. As president of the Twin Falls and the Idaho State Business and Professional Women's Clubs, Mrs. Langdon would be honored as the Idaho Business Woman of the Year. Marian Langdon, who would also serve as president of the Soroptimist Club and the Twentieth Century Club in the 1980s, would retire in 1986 after running the business alone for forty years.

Governments Got Involved

Morale was at its lowest by 1932. The dust bowl was sending thousands of emigrants to Idaho, and Twin Falls County's unemployment exceeded 30 percent. Several hundred homeless people inhabited Rock Creek Canyon making shelters of wooden crates, tin sheds, and caves dug out of dirt and rock. The County Commission was hard pressed to remove this "shantytown" since the county was going bankrupt and had only script to give to the poor for food and coal. One man who was gleaning plums was arrested, convicted, and sentenced to one month in jail (possibly a blessing). The poor people simply cleaned out Detweiler-Nye's box car of coal.

> *Teachers and teachers' salaries were cut, 41 percent of the budget went for charity.*
> —Dr. Jim Gentry

Twin Falls turned Democratic with the rest of the country in 1932, and Franklin D. Roosevelt was elected president. That same year Paul Bickel died and John E. Hayes succeeded him as city engineer. F.D.R. put his New Deal program to work through the Work Projects Administration (WPA), and Mayor R. E. Bobier delegated Hayes to administer the WPA funds. Hayes supervised construction of a road into Rock Creek Canyon by jobless men, many of whom lived in the canyon's shantytown.

Twin Falls County went broke in 1933 purchasing property with a hotel—formerly used by sugar factory employees—for the County Poor Farm, which the WPA would build in 1940. In 1935 the Idaho legislature funded the construction of the Migrant Labor Camp on Washington Street one mile south of the Singing Bridge.

The 18th Amendment was repealed in 1933 ending Prohibition. Twin Falls had a new mayor that year: Duncan M. Johnston, a local jeweler who would give the city a shock five years later. In 1935 Twin Falls began to come out of the Great Depression.

Chapter 11

Coming Out of the Depression, 1935–1941

The Majestic Pharmacy—in the [Perrine] *hotel building—was a required morning stop for a soft drink, the newsstand for the latest magazine, Wray's Café for a more substantial repast, and the Perrine Barber Shop.* —Gus Kelker recalled 1935, the year he arrived in Twin Falls

Twin Falls Dug Itself Out of a Hole in 1935

Through President Roosevelt's New Deal programs, farm prices and construction began to pick up, unemployment started to drop, and the county's solvency was restored. The Twin Falls County Fair and Twin Falls County Public Health, which were shut down in 1932 and 1933 respectively, were reinstated and funded again. Harmon Park got a swimming pool through the WPA, and City Park got a new lava rock band shell through the Idaho Employment Relief Act.

City planning got moving under Mayor Duncan Johnston with a new Zoning Commission and a new Community Planning Commission. The Fire Department was increased to eight firemen and the police force grew to seven patrolmen. Officers Kenneth Barclay and Craig Bracken, son of a previous mayor F. F. Bracken, were among the patrolmen hired by Mayor Johnston, as was Chief of Police Howard Gillette.

Social activities resumed. The Perrines invited everyone from the county for Sunday picnics and potlucks at Blue Lakes: there were "Missouri picnics," "Nebraska picnics," and others. Saturday nights were so busy with people coming to town from all the outlying towns that grocery stores had to stay open until midnight, even as late as 2 A.M., as shoppers waited until last minute to grocery-shop before going home. There were dance halls with live bands, "but mostly, adults just visited with everyone and the kids ran around." Distilleries were up to speed just three years after the repeal of Prohibition. Downtown Twin Falls blossomed with saloons and nine houses of prostitution. Slot machines were allowed; city government got half the take.

> *Saturday night was booming. The town was really jumping then; now it's dead.*
> —A. Wiley Dodds (1999)

Education got a boost. Only two Republicans ran in the 1936 Idaho elections, and both won: William E. Borah remained a United States senator, and Doris Stradley—recommended by *The Idaho Evening Times* as the only "honest" Republican on the ballot—became the Twin Falls County superintendent of schools. Stradley had been an excellent 1- and 2-room school teacher for ten years, supporting her two children after her husband's death in 1932 from illness caused by poison gas in World War I. Local Chapter Five of the Disabled American Veterans, or DAV, would be named for H. A. Stradley. As superintendent, Doris Stradley did the achievement testing in

both the town and rural schools and took audio-visual materials to the rural schools as well.

> *These were usually 1- or 2-room schools for the first eight grades. . . . The younger children learned by listening to the older ones and all helped each other.*
> —Emily Tverdy

Twin Falls got two new schools in 1938: Bickel Elementary and a new addition on the 1909 Lincoln Elementary. The junior and senior high schools were reorganized.

The Twentieth Century Club began a campaign in 1935 for a WPA grant of $22,000 for a library building. This was approved in 1938, and a matching bond issue added another $27,500. The Benoit property on Second Street E across from City Park was purchased, and there the new Twin Falls Public Library was constructed in 1939 to contain its 17,400 books. Andrew McQuaker, architect for the handsome brick building, designed the skewed compass rose that was inlaid in the floor at the front entrance to indicate the angle on which the townsite was set.

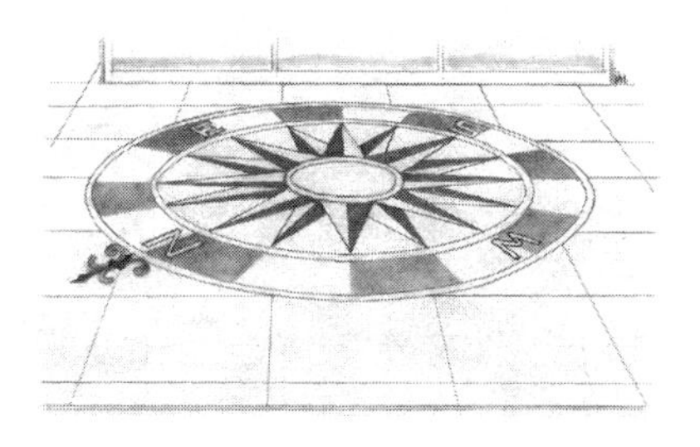

Live concert music got a boost. Back in the 1920s, live stage entertainment was replaced by movies with sound tracks. But even musical movies could not replace a national appetite for live performance that Vaudeville, Chautauqua, and traveling minstrel shows had created. The appetite gap was filled in 1927 by a unique eastern plan to first raise the money, then hire the artists. The result was Community Concerts. A local chapter was organized in Twin Falls in 1937 to bring in small professional music groups such as string quartets and ballets. Over the years, Twin Falls lovers of fine music enjoyed such artists as the Von Trapp Family Singers, Leontyne Price (in 1957), and Three Hits and a Miss (in 2001).

> *Community Concerts is the oldest performing-arts-presenting organization in Twin Falls. It was then, and is still, a volunteer organization. There is no paid staff. We are people who want national and world-class artists, and we get together and make it happen.*
> —Dave Nelson, Sav-Mor Drugs (2000)

The best part was the receptions held after the concerts in the homes of the board members where we got to meet the visiting artists.

—Marty Mead, new member in 1959

Digging Out Meant Turnovers, Transitions, and Newcomers

After twenty-five years in the business, the Riley Sisters, who purchased pheasant skins from bird hunters, sold their millinery shop to Reed's Millinery. Coe M. Price purchased the Twin Falls Hardware—the town's first, established in 1904 by Roy W. Gager—and the business became Price Hardware. Also in 1935 the Twin Falls Building and Loan Association, which was established in 1916, became the First Federal Savings and Loan Association of Twin Falls.

In the 1920s Benoit's Blue Lakes Bottling Company—built in 1908 on Shoshone Street near the passenger depot—became Deigart's Depot Service and Texaco Station where railroad crews could get sandwiches. This station was sold in 1935 to the Mays family who transformed it into the Depot Grill with eleven stools and 24-hour service by a staff of four. The Grill accommodated the workers and passengers on the "Gallopin' Goose" train from Salt Lake City and the employees from the flour mill next door.

We last saw trumpeter Fred Sanger clerking for two years in the Perrine Hotel lobby before returning to the university at Moscow to finish college and get his law degree. Fred returned again to Twin Falls in 1935, and the next year, he took a civil service exam for postal employees. He passed the exam and was hired at the U.S. Post Office as a "temporary indefinite substitute clerk carrier." After three months, Fred was appointed to a permanent clerk position at the rate of $1,700 a year, an enormous salary.

I was making more money than the prosecuting attorney!

—Fred Sanger

In his thirty-four years at the post office, Fred Sanger would become tour foreman, superintendent of mails, and finally postmaster. During all those years, Fred would continue to play his trumpet in the weekly summer concerts in City Park along with the other twenty-five or thirty members of the City Band. In 2004, when Twin Falls would celebrate its hundredth birthday, Fred would celebrate living ninety-four of those years, and Cynthia, his wife of sixty-two years, would celebrate living ninety-two years.

Jack Frederickson came to Twin Falls in 1936 to open and manage a new kind of ice cream store for Ray C. Green of Salt Lake City. Business wasn't as good as Green had expected. After the slow summer of 1937, Mr. Green gave Jack the option to buy the business, and on 1 October Jack owned Frederickson's Ice Cream Store (now on Second Street E). Jack Frederickson bought new machinery and started making the Frederickson's Chocolates that would make Twin Falls famous.

> *My father had always been in the candy business, and he convinced me I should make candy to carry the store through "the cold months" . . . when ice cream did not sell.* —Jack Frederickson

The Sav-Mor Drug chain established a store in Twin Falls in 1938 (still at 139 Main Avenue W today). Two years later, Al Nelson became a partner in what would become a family business and "the oldest family-owned drug store in town." Around the corner at 215 Shoshone S, Red's Trading Post was established in Bradley's old harness and saddle shop.

Pioneer Stickers kept moving up. The Detweiler Brothers were then into heating and plumbing by public demand. The volume of their business required a move to 131 Main Avenue E in 1935, the year Harry was fatally injured in an auto accident. Claude and George continued in the business and made a second move in 1937 to 140 Second Avenue N (now Standard Printing) to accommodate their new electrical wiring and sheet metal departments.

In 1937 Brizee Metal Works installed the first residential oil furnace at the (now Historic) Burkholder home at 335 Blue Lakes Boulevard N.

> *It's still crankin' out the BTUs just fine* [in 2003].
> —Bill Kyle, Burkholder Residence owner since 1987

The Babbels built their first plant at 124 Third Street S in 1938 and went from tailoring into dry cleaning. They called their business Babbel's Clothing Clinic.

Mrs. Ella White moved her business in 1939 from a building storefront to her newly constructed White Mortuary "Chapel by the Park" located at 136 Fourth Avenue E across from City Park. Mrs. White's daughter Frances and her husband Hugh Phillips then bought the business and retained the name. The Phillipses would operate the business until 1980, sell it to Jerry D. Holman and Ronald Hamilton, and retire. In 1988 Mr. Hamilton would retire and Mr. Holman would become sole owner of White Mortuary.

Scandal and Tragedy Hit a Small Town

Twin Falls was rocked by a murder and scandal on 24 May 1938. The lifeless body of George L. Olson, a diamond salesman from Salt Lake City, was discovered in a car parked behind the Park Hotel, and half a million dollars in gems was missing. Police Chief Gillette investigated. The clues pointed to a prominent citizen of Twin Falls: former mayor Duncan Johnston who owned a jewelry store on Main Avenue E and was the last to see the salesman alive.

OFFICER CRAIG BRACKEN

The police chief and an electrician took a room at the Rogerson Hotel and obtained a key to Bertha Campbell's Dress Shop, both establishments being in the same block with Johnston's store. The two men went into the common basement to "bug" the jewelry store. There they happened upon the cache of gems wrapped in a towel hidden in a recess in the basement wall. Officer Craig Bracken was assigned to a stake-out and he caught the ex-mayor. Johnston was tried and convicted and sent to prison. Also arrested was an employee of Johnston's; William LaVonde was a desk sergeant at the police station, which was in the same building as the mayor's office. But not enough evidence was found to convict this accomplice, and he skipped town.

Tragically, Officer Bracken died in the line of duty on 8 May 1939. Two bums from Nevada stole a car and robbed a service station. They were spotted by Officers Bracken and Barclay who then followed and stopped the suspects. Shots were fired on both sides; both miscreants were wounded, and one of them wounded Officer Bracken who died the next day. The murderer got a sentence of life in prison where he spent twenty years; his accomplice got seven years.

Historical Update: Sixty-one years later on 20 January 2000, the Twin Falls Police Department awarded the Medal of Honor posthumously to the fallen forty-five-year-old policeman, the only one of any Twin Falls force to die in the line of duty. The presentation was made to Craig Bracken's daughter Virginia Bracken O'Dell and son Frank Bracken.

Getting Back to Normal

Joe Koehler—owner of the Roxy Theater, active in the Shriners, Commander of Veterans of Foreign Wars—became mayor in 1939, and World War I veteran Harry Benoit became city attorney. Koehler put his support behind the movements for a municipal airport, for a Twin Falls Housing Authority, and to get the Cowboy baseball team. Twin Falls did become "Home of the Cowboys" in 1939 when the New York Yankees sent one of its expansion teams. Adult admission for the games played in the new Jaycees' Field next to Harmon Park was five cents, and the Cowboys had free tickets to all the shows at the mayor's Roxy Theater, until it's sale in 1958. The Cowboys baseball team was one of four Idaho teams in the Pioneer League, a member of the National Association of Professional Baseball Leagues; this league also had two Utah and two Montana teams. These Cowboys would continue to call Twin Falls home until 1971 when, by then, television would have lured away the ballpark audience.

There were more signs of getting back to normal:

> *Golfers scattered as the monoplane swooped over the Twin Falls Golf Course, touched down on a fairway, and rolled safely to a stop. The resident pro came on the run ready to chew out whoever had pulled off such an irresponsible stunt. The pilot leaned out the window and grinned, "Do you sell cokes here?" he* [Gus Kelker] *asked.*
>
> —Denise Turner, *The Times-News* staff

To kick off this drab town's first decade, Twin Falls had the prankster Sam Hamilton; to bring it out of the Great Depression, Twin Falls had Gus Kelker. A photographer, newspaperman, and Idaho history buff, Gus would live to age eighty-one in 1993.

> *Kelker's business card said it all: Epigrammist, tiger-tamer, bar-emptier, itch-scratcher, war-fighter, assassination-plotter, and revolution-starter, to name a few.* —Steve Crump, *The Times-News* staff

The County Poor Farm did not last long.

> *If you didn't work hard, someone would have been right behind you taking your job.* —Stan Day (1990)

The WPA built the County Poor Farm just east of the sugar factory on 3700 N in 1940. To be as self-sufficient as possible and little burden on the county, indigent residents raised their own food until local food retailers complained that this was competition with their business. The Poor Farm would be abandoned late in the 1950s and a sugar factory manager would

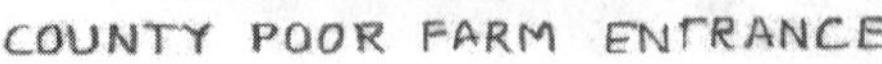

plan its destruction. But Amalgamated's president Allen Lipman would declare "This is history" and save the lava rock sheds, the arched lava rock courtyard entryway, and the walls with its two historic plaques.

The Migrant Labor Camp gave many a new start.

> *The first labor camp, with wooden tent-cabins and old fashioned outhouses used in the '20s and '30s, was at the railroad crossing on the sugar factory property (and since filled in with lime). In about 1935 the camp was moved to Washington Street.* —Otto Florence Jr.

One mile south of the Singing Bridge on Washington Street the state built the Migrant Labor Camp. There a laborer could rent a 2-room shelter for four dollars a week, or he could work it out if he didn't have the money. The work was seasonal: harvesting fruit, sugar beets, and potatoes by hand. The migrants were mostly "Okies" from Oklahoma and "Arkies" from Arkansas.

The Meyers family of six came from Denver, Colorado, to the Labor Camp in 1940 and rented two units. Johnny, fourteen years old, and his brother thinned sugar beets, pitched hay, planted lawns, peddled fruit, did anything they could find to help with the rent. That fall they saw a farmer on his tractor pushing over his apple trees full of big Rome Beauties; he said he couldn't afford to harvest them for the two cents a bushel the cider mill paid. For that price the farmer let the Meyers boys have all the apples they could gather, which they sold for $1.00 to $1.25 a bushel.

> *Working a 4-hour day for the WPA gave two men a job—and survival.* —Johnny Meyers (2000)

In Denver, Dad Meyers had worked at the Elitch's Gardens. In Twin Falls he got his big break with a job planting the grass at Pioneer Square (near present Latham Motors) that paid $120, and Meyers Landscaping was established. Johnny would branch off on his own in 1945 and carry on the family business.

Finally, "toll-free" signaled that the Great Depression was history. The state of Idaho purchased the Twin Falls-Jerome Intercounty Bridge and removed the toll in 1940. Autos clogged the bridge from both sides of the river in one tremendous ceremony involving the conjoined cities.

> *Following the speaking program, old autos were run off the cliffs on each side of the canyon and crashed to bits on the huge lava rocks below. . . . Throwing over a replica of the toll house went on as scheduled . . . the structure fell apart before it struck the water.*
>
> —*The Idaho Evening Times*

Twin Falls was back to normal.

As war clouds gathered over Europe, Toby Cagle's little Twin Falls Airport (one dirt runway a mile south of the present Joslin Field) prepared pilots in case the U.S.A. got involved in the conflict. Instructor Jack Wise offered flight scholarships to the highest-scoring 10 percent of the trainees. Twin Falls native June Skinner won a scholarship and got her private pilot's license.

> *I was in the civilian pilot training program in 1939 and studied like the Dickens for that scholarship. But I didn't pass the army physical, so I stayed on as a ground school instructor.* —Art Frantz (2003)

Chapter 12

World War II Years, 1941–1945

On 7 December 1941—just when the community of Twin Falls had pulled itself out of the Great Depression by overcoming low farm prices, lost credit and savings, unemployment and poverty—the "Japs" (Japanese Empire) bombed Pearl Harbor (in U.S. Territory of Hawaii), plunging the United States into the worldwide conflict. World War II was called "WWII."

Profound Effects Were Felt

> *The draft took men as old as forty—eighteen to forty. That was half our men.*
> —Edith Robertson

Families were disrupted by the loss of husbands and fathers, brothers, cousins, and uncles, even sisters and daughters to the military. Many wives joined their husbands at army and navy bases, and when their men were shipped overseas, these women returned home to live with relatives. Twin Falls men and women moved to the West Coast to work in defense plants where ships and airplanes were built.

> *I worked in communications at Bremerton Navy Yard and sent coded messages to the ships at sea.*
> —Ruby Lierman, volunteer, Twin Falls County Historical Society Museum (2003)

The war effort involved everyone. Adults bought "war bonds," children sold and bought "war stamps" in their schools. Along with exempt and older men, women on the homefront held Civil Defense meetings, drills, and patrols. Twin Falls women knitted hats, scarves, gloves, mittens, and sewed jackets and quilts for servicemen; collected *LIFE* magazines for the USO (United Service Organization); sponsored Red Cross classes, prepared first aid kits, and rolled bandages; packed "care packages" and Christmas boxes for men overseas.

The rationing of sugar, coffee, butter, meat, shoes, tires, and gas, was hardly new—"rationing" had become a way of life during the depression—and women saved up rationed sugar all year to do their fall canning. Making purchases with stamps or coupons from a ration book was just another way of budgeting already limited resources. Since the conserving of resources was common in the depression, drives to collect paper, scrap iron, tin and aluminum, bacon grease to be used in ammunition, and milkweed to go into life jackets were simply new ways to conserve on a community-wide scale. It wasn't called "recycling" then, but that was practiced as the patriotic thing to do.

Shortages became commonplace. Twin Falls women adapted to the shortage of nylon stockings (which had just replaced silk and didn't bag at the knees, so hemlines went up) by using leg make-up the color of stockings. Some ladies carefully drew a "seam" up the back of their legs (seamless hose were bound to follow). With a shortage of razor blades, women "shaved" their legs with sandpaper. Hair styles went romantic as young women let their bobbed hair grow for glamour photos to send to their absent hubbies and sweethearts.

Growing one's own food was nothing new around Twin Falls, and city folks with a patch of yard on the sunny side of the house planted "Victory gardens." Vacant lots were made available for neighbors to garden together and raise vegetables for their families because of the need for America to feed the armed services from its larger food basket.

The U.S. Government Built Camps and Installations

Hunt Camp was a big mistake in that civil liberties got squashed in the name of national security.

> *Victims of wartime hysteria, these people, two thirds of whom were American citizens, lived a bleak and humiliating life in tar paper barracks behind barbed wire and under armed guard.*
>
> —Sign at the vacated Hunt Camp site

The Minidoka Relocation Center, built near Eden in Jerome County, was known locally as Hunt Camp since the nearest post office was at Hunt,

Idaho. Early in 1942 the U.S. military uprooted ten to twelve thousand Japanese-Americans from the Seattle and Portland areas and sent them to this 73-acre camp on 33,000 acres of desert. Here they would live under crude conditions and fend for themselves; some were transferred on to nine other similar camps.

> *I was fifteen years old, my brother was about twenty. There were a lot of kids and we enjoyed it. There was no work—just loiter, play, and eat.*
>
> —George Kawamoto (2001)

Interned at Hunt were two Oregon families who would make a place in Twin Falls history: the Kawamotos from Portland and the Ishidas of Salem. As soon as the Kawamotos arrived, the boys, George and Kay, contracted out to the farms to work the fall harvests.

> *We stayed at the Paul labor camp and dug potatoes on 120 acres in Eden and were paid by the sack. That harvest took twenty days. Then we stayed at the Filer fairgrounds, had meals at the Filer Café, and topped beets, all by hand. We made more money on the farms than our parents who found work at Hunt in the kitchen or the hospital or raising hogs on the farms at Hunt; they made $20 a month. After the harvest, I returned to Hunt for school.* —George Kawamoto

> *. . . I would pick up some teenage Hunt internees walking along the road, drop them at the snack bar and pick some up on my return. . . . They could have been some of my high school friends, talking about sports, girls, and school.* —Cecil Leon Rice (2003)

Kay volunteered for military service and was rejected. Then just as the war was ending, Kay was drafted. The irony was that while Hunt had one of the highest rates of voluntary military service, these patriotic Japanese-American servicemen had to visit their families living in the internment camps. Of the three hundred volunteers from Hunt Camp, 120 were trained at Camp Shelby, Mississippi, and then sent to Italy as members of the famous all-Japanese-American 442nd Infantry Combat Unit, the most decorated in U.S. military history. The 120-member Hunt squad suffered eighty-two casualties; seventy-six were killed in action.

Inland Japanese-Americans were not interned during the war. Tom Koto, born of Twin Falls pioneers and living in Shoshone, volunteered early in 1941 for one year in the army but served for four and a half years.

> *My cousin was in the service with Tom Koto. We met when Tom came home on furlough. . . . We were married fifty-five years when Tom died in January 2002.* —Matsuye Ishida Koto, Hunt Camp internee

Like the Kawamoto brothers, Tom and "Mats" Koto would make their home in Twin Falls after the war.

There were other installations in the area. Near Paul, Idaho, the U.S. government built a German-prisoner-of-war camp, and there were complaints that those enemies of our country got better treatment than our American citizens interned at Hunt Camp. A Navy hospital took over Sun Valley for convalescent servicemen. The Mountain Home Air Force Base opened in 1944.

Hotel and Ballroom Businesses Boomed

During the war, all hotels had priority on scarce and rationed commodities like meat and sugar. In Jenny Hoops Stewart's Rogerson Restaurant a meal for seventy-five cents included shrimp cocktail, T-bone steak, mashed potatoes and gravy, vegetable, dinner salad, pie and coffee. Jenny observed that customers would put three or four spoons of sugar in their coffee and never stir it. In the spirit of patriotism Jenny hung a sign which read "Limit—one spoonful of sugar per cup and stir like HELL!"

When the draft hit, Fred and William Hoops, owners of Hoops Construction Company and the Rogerson Hotel, purchased the Park Hotel and then sold it to their sister Jenny.

Many of the Park Hotel employees came from the Hunt Concentration [sic] Camp during the war.—Lynn Jaynes and Jenny Stewart (1990)

All Jenny's employees worked 12-hour shifts through the war when the Park Hotel did its best business. So many convalescent servicemen came from Sun Valley on week-ends that they packed the Twin Falls hotels. Even the lobby of the Park was set up with cots, and single rooms held four or more at $1.50 per night, or $2.00 with private bath. "You could wingding all night long in the town's clubs."

Stanley Soule, the owner of KTFI and Radioland Ballroom in the Herriott Building, died suddenly in 1937 and his sister Florence M. Gardner took over the reins. In 1940 she had Bobier Company build the Radio Rondevoo at 241 Main Avenue W with a ballroom dance floor and stage downstairs and offices and a large radio studio upstairs. On Saturday nights through World War II it was "Live from the KTFI Ballroom" with big name bands like Tommy Dorsey, Glenn Miller, Lawrence Welk, as well as local bands.

One of those local bands was called "Melody Skeemers." Wayne Skeem, a Castleford High School sophomore, got up a band with six boys and two girls. The group was so good, they played every Saturday night at the Radioland Ballroom from 1939 to 1942 and at the Radio Rondevoo Ballroom from 1940 until 1944 when the Army inducted the young men to fight for their country. Soule's old ballroom at Radioland would became the Rollerdrome Skating Rink in the 1950s.

Twin Falls Companies Had Government Contracts

World War II gave the Hoops Construction Company government contracts to build airstrips and roads in the state, including the roads at the Minidoka Relocation Center. In the early 1900s German-born Wilhelm M. Hoops brought his family—including Fred, William, and Jenny—via New York, Illinois, and Wyoming to Rock Creek, Idaho. There he tried farming, got discouraged, and turned to construction where "there was money to be made." Wilhelm started the Hoops Construction Company with canal-and-road building and city-and-farmland clearing and leveling. The Hoops family company went from one hundred horses for grading and moving earth with fresnos to modern construction of state highways in Nevada, Wyoming, and Idaho. Hoops Construction Company built four of Idaho's first overpasses.

Another company with government contracts was the Detweiler Brothers. George Detweiler described their job at the half-billion-dollar Glasgow installation: "We were the first construction firm in the Glasgow Air Force Base and the last to leave. [The base was] hardly ever used." Through World War II, the Detweiler Brothers had seventeen U.S. government contracts going on at one time in Army and Air Force bases in Washington, Utah, Wyoming, Nevada, and North Carolina.

Businesses Had to Make Wartime Adjustments

Clarence Allen of Sterling Jewelry, whom we saw squeak through the depression by processing Snake River gold, was hit during the war by a federal luxury tax which made quality merchandise harder to get. Allen's two sons went into the service. Howard entered the Marines in 1943. Charles was drafted in 1945 after working as paymaster for Morrison-Knudson Company in the construction of the Minidoka Relocation Center and for Detweiler Brothers in defense work in Utah. Clarence died in 1944 leaving the store to Mrs. Allen and her sister until after the war when her sons would return to the family business.

~

The Maytag business of E. E. White who bought Wilson-Bates in 1935 was directly affected by the OPA (Office of Price Administration) during WWII. The OPA not only rationed the purchase of major appliances but audited mark-up percentages in its attempt to put a crimp in "black market" activities. White was offered many under-the-counter sales, but these he strictly turned down. The reputation that E. E. White preserved during the War would always be appreciated at Wilson-Bates.

> *The Whites might be offered $500 for a Maytag washer which would sell for less than $100.* —Donna Scott (1990)

S. Leslie Crowley, a Walgreen Drug Store employee from Salt Lake City, arrived in Twin Falls with his family in December 1941 to see Trolinger's Pharmacy for the first time. Crowley came with an opportunity to buy the pharmacy, which he did the following month. (The name would be retained until 1961 when son Robert would change it to Crowley Pharmacy.) The pharmacy was on the main floor of the 3-story Booth Building on Main Avenue S; the floors above had doctors' offices, the Twin Falls Business School, a dance studio, and a camera shop. In the front of the pharmacy was a soda fountain where a shopper could enjoy a twenty-five cent soda or a ten cent glass of root beer as well as a hot lunch prepared in the basement kitchen. During the war, tobacco and film were also rationed. People lined up at Crowley's doors before the store opened, and by the end of the day, the rationed supplies were gone.

> *Downtown was the place for mile-long parades and holiday festivities. On weekends shoppers filled the streets and there was more than enough business. Everything and everybody was downtown.*
>
> —S. Leslie Crowley (1990)

When C. C. Dudley, who homesteaded eighty acres of the Twin Falls Tract in 1908, was driven from his farm by a ruinous hailstorm in 1924, he moved his family into town and opened an insurance business. As C.C. traveled throughout southern Idaho selling insurance, he became interested in photography as a hobby. People came to Dudley's home to have their pictures taken. During WWII many servicemen and their brides requested wedding pictures. Gas rationing made traveling very difficult for the insurance salesman, and before the war ended, Dudley was in the photography business.

> *The studio has always been at the original location* [in the Dudley home] *on Blue Lakes Boulevard near North Five Points.*
>
> —Clarence Dudley (1990)

After serving as a technician in the Army Air Force, C. C. Dudley's son Clarence went to college to study music. This endeavor would be cut short by C.C.'s first heart attack in 1949. Clarence would come home to help out with the business and stay to continue in the Dudley tradition of quality photography after C.C.'s death in 1965. Clarence would not abandon his love of music. In 1985 he would become music director at the First Methodist Church, a position he would hold until retirement in 2000, adding his own choral compositions to the choir's repertory.

Another loss during the war was Harry Brizee. Brother Leland purchased the shop from Harry's widow in 1943. Leland and his wife Elizabeth worked many long hours to keep the shop open when help was scarce.

The City Honored Its Heroes

Less than a year after the attack on Pearl Harbor, a B-17 bomber carrying a young Twin Falls airman was shot down over the Solomon Islands, and that radioman Sgt. Raymond R. Joslin lost his life. Mayor Joe Koehler, who was pushing for an airport for Twin Falls, thought it would be appropriate to name a new airfield for Twin Falls's first Air Force serviceman to die in World War II. The following year, Twin Falls won the approval of the CAA (Civil Aeronautics Administration) for the airport and it would be named Joslin Field.

> *My brother Raymond joined the Air Corps before the war and was in the flyover for President Roosevelt's* [third] *inauguration.*
>
> —Joyce Joslin Harding (1998)

Ira Burton Perrine quietly passed away on 2 October 1943 at the age of eighty-two and was buried at his beloved Blue Lakes Ranch. Bert had seen forty years of growth of his city from dust-to-mud stagecoach roads to pavement for airplanes. In 1984 nurseryman Johnny Meyers would acquire Perrine's original stagecoach, which was badly deteriorated, and restore it to mint condition. Johnny would use it for many civic occasions including

I.B. PERRINE

having it on display at the airport terminal in 2000 as a Twin Falls Centennial icon honoring both the Father of Twin Falls and the city's history of transportation. In 2001, at the age of seventy-five, a much admired Johnny Meyers would suffer a fatal heart attack in his barn beside his beloved stagecoach.

The War Ended

V-J Day (Victory in Japan) on 2 September 1945 marked the end of World War II. People in Twin Falls rushed to the Radio Rondevoo to listen to reports over the national networks and to celebrate. The Japanese-Americans, credited with saving Magic Valley crops during the war, left Hunt Camp to return to their home states where, in many cases, their property had been confiscated and sold. Many had nothing to return to but old friends to help them start over.

> *While interned at Minidoka, Japanese-Americans cleared and cultivated 950 acres of inhospitable land and constructed the ditches and canals needed to irrigate them. Beginning in 1947, these lands were divided* [by the Bureau of Reclamation] *into smaller farms and given to World War II veterans whose names were drawn by lottery or auctioned to the highest bidder. Issei (Japanese who had emigrated to America; they comprised one-third of the internees) were excluded from both the lottery and sale of the farms as they were not allowed to own property or become naturalized citizens until 1952.*
>
> —National Park Service brochure

Chapter 13

The Post–War Years, 1945–1960

Agriculture took a leap forward when one of the largest aquifers in the world containing as much water as Lake Erie was discovered underlying about ten thousand square miles of southern Idaho. The waters of this Snake River Plain Aquifer flow slowly to the Thousand Springs region where they emerge and replace the Snake River waters that were diverted for surface irrigation. Recharge of this aquifer comes from snowmelt and rainfall on the mountains to the north and east plus seepage from the Upper Snake River and irrigation canals. The first sprinkler-irrigation systems drawing water from the aquifer appeared in Magic Valley farmlands in 1950.

The American Dream Came True

The most important change after World War II came because of the GI Bill of Rights with its VA home loans: We became a country of homeowners.

—Old Timer

The American dream was always to own "a little cottage with a white picket fence." That dream came true after World War II as veterans were guaranteed no-down-payment home loans through the Veterans Administration (VA). The GI (Government Issue) Bill provided for "service points" (educational credits) which sent the first generation of "GIs" off to campuses for the higher education or training many could not have afforded otherwise. So began the trend away from rural farm jobs and into cities for the higher wages that would make affordable the mortgage payments on that little cottage.

With funding from the GI Bill, veterans flooded the colleges and universities, large and small. These institutions grew rapidly adding courses to their curricula. Some small colleges that did not offer what enough GIs were looking for lost out in the competition and folded. Such was Idaho's Albion State Normal School which closed in 1951. For fifty-nine years Albion State had produced the core—if not the majority—of Magic Valley teachers that would extend into the 1960s.

Lower Education Took a Hit

As early as 1947 *The Times-News* reported that local teachers were receiving the lowest salaries in the Western United States, which didn't help the teacher shortage that developed after Albion Normal School closed. One low-paid Twin Falls teacher was Norman Herrett who came to Idaho from South Dakota in 1941 to teach shop at the high school. He and his wife, Lillie, developed a lapidary and jewelry business on the side. In 1946 they built their jewelry store at 1220 Kimberly Road and Norman quit teaching. Six years later, Herrett constructed his first observatory: a canvas-covered enclosure in his back yard to house a small telescope that he had designed and built. Still interested in education he invited students and others to star-gazing sessions.

Norman Herrett's project grew to include an observatory with two large permanent telescopes and a planetarium that attracted national attention. Astronomers and planetarium directors came to see Norman mimic the night skies using small motors, lights, and switches. The Herretts also began raising tropical fish and birds, which they showed to local school groups. They became interested in American Indians, and when the Herretts returned from numerous trips to Central and South America, they replaced the fish and birds with Indian artifacts.

Another teacher affected after the war was Doris Stradley. A 1948 Idaho State law "forced consolidation" of rural schools by providing free transportation for rural school children. The result was the demise of the 1- and 2-room schools. In Twin Falls County twenty-five little rural schools that had "served as the focal points of their communities" were consolidated into seven districts.

> *It was the beginning of the end of any feeling of community in their neighborhoods.*
> —Doris Stradley

In 1951, when a new County Hospital was built, Doris Stradley's office of the county superintendent of schools was moved from the County Courthouse to the old County Hospital. A new Twin Falls High School was built on Filer Avenue E in 1954, and the old school building, which also housed the junior high, became O'Leary Junior High School. In 1959 the position that Mrs. Stradley had held for twenty-three years was phased out, and the invincible lady went back to teaching. She would retire in 1961 at age sixty-four.

Medical Facilities and Services Expanded

Four physicians returning from military service in 1946 built the Twin Falls Clinic and Hospital which opened the following year. Privately owned and operated, for profit and tax-paying, "the Clinic" provided ten hospital beds as well as offices for its founding doctors: Elwood T. Rees, Joseph W. Marshall, David A. McClusky, and Earl C. Jensen. In the decades to follow, the Clinic would grow to forty-four beds with a surgery wing, an 8-bed intensive care unit, a full service laboratory, an X-ray department, and an oncology department.

The opening of the Clinic was timely, but the blizzards that hit the Twin Falls area in 1948 stranded many would-be patients. With below-zero temperatures, high winds, and snow drifts as high as ten feet in places, trains and hundreds of motorists were stranded. Farmers took in snow-bound motorists and neighbors. Schools and the airport were closed. Means to get medicines, food, and hay to isolated locations had to be devised using a temporary airstrip. A ski-plane took doctors to emergencies. Without trains to bring coal, and with trucks unable to bring in milk from farms, serious shortages of fuel and milk developed. Rural towns and the National Guard worked together. Happily, no loss of life was reported.

> *BLM helped to get supplies to us as well as furnishing a large truck to take us to the community hall for a Christmas party. This was the only social event of that lonely winter.*
> —Lois Ritchie (Brannon), homesteading at Hunt

Four years after the Clinic was built, the Twin Falls County Commission approved the construction of a new County Hospital. The 60-bed Magic Valley Memorial Hospital was built in 1951 next to the old 36-bed hospital.

In May 1947 Idaho's legislature created voluntary health districts and allocated state general funds to cover 70 percent of the cost; the counties and cities would cover the rest.

> *The local health unit* [Southcentral District Health] *which serves the eight Magic Valley counties is by far the largest in the state and employs approximately half of the personnel of the Idaho State Department of Public Health.* —*The Times-News* (1957)

In 1953 political discord resulted in Twin Falls County pulling out of the Southcentral District Health; Twin Falls City stayed. When all of the county commissioners lost their seats in 1957, the County, with a new commission, rejoined the District.

Into the 1950s the medical community continued to wait until afflicted children were five or six years old before encouraging parents to send them to deaf and blind school. In 1960 Merle Stoddard—a war widow with four children and a master's degree in speech pathology and audiology—independently started the Easter Seals Program. Her purpose was to educate both the public and doctors to the importance of working with children from birth to catch hearing and speech disorders. Merle went door to door raising funds, and the community responded. KMVT gave prime time for promotion of the program. Western Music Bands gave concerts to raise money. The Rotary Club built a house off Locust Street for the Easter Seals Program, and the Twentieth Century Club donated furniture and therapy equipment. Success was assured by the hundreds of volunteers like Rudy Williamson, Buzz Langdon, Art Frantz, and Hank Wills, and some very supportive physicians like Dr. Ben Katz.

Historical Update: After twenty years, in 1981, a "tired" Merle quit and closed her program's doors. Since then, many private speech therapy clinics opened in Twin Falls to take Merle's place. Today the MVRMC boasts its Outpatient Pediatric Therapy Facility with a staff of eleven that treats patients from birth to twenty-one years for all the problems of cerebral palsy and speech and motor coordination. Tired? At this writing (2003), Merle at eighty-four is still actively teaching dancing, touring with her Stoddard's Tappers, and writing her monthly Letter to the Editor of *The Times-News* to give a piece of her mind to certain owners of Confined Animal Feeding Operations for the health hazards they create.

Amenities Proliferated

In 1945 a 9-hole, riverside golf course was built. Back in 1922, the articles of incorporation for a Blue Lakes Country Club were filed by A. L. Swim, L. L. Breckenridge, E. J. Ostrander, and L. A. Chapin. However, Hortense Perrine refused to sell the ranch. Twenty-two years later, son Burton Perrine and his wife Emerald met with Bert Sweet, Claude Detweiler, W. G. Swim, and C. R. Nelson representing the corporation. The younger Perrines granted an option-to-lease for a term of fifty years for a sum of $3,600 per year, and the golf course was built. In 1964 Blue Lakes Country Club would purchase the lease-option property for $60,000, build a new clubhouse to replace the one that burned down, and expand to eighteen holes.

A new airport was built. In 1946 Twin Falls voters passed a $250,000 bond election to match the funds that the CAA had approved during the War for an airport. For roughly twenty years, private planes had used a landing strip on Kimberly Road (where United Oil is today), then used Toby Cagle's dirt runway, which was south of the location chosen for a new airport. In the spring of 1948 Twin Falls opened its 640-acre Joslin Field complete with a fire station and a Diamond-T fire truck. United Airlines began service on 1 May 1948 with the DC3.

And the food was good! —Edith Robertson

In the 1970s, Hughes Air West would provide jet service with its two DC9 models that would carry 83 and 103 passengers. Air Idaho would provide local service to Boise, Sun Valley, Burley, and Salt Lake City.

Three new parks were added. When Twin Falls was fifty years old in 1954 and with a population of almost twenty thousand, the city had only four parks: City Park (1904), Drury Park (1917), Harmon Park (1926) to which Jaycee Field was added in 1938, and South Park (originally Highland Park, 1943). The City Council created an 8-member Twin Falls Parks and Recreation Commission ("Parks and Rec"). But the new commission had little money for new parks, so it made a request for land donations. Several community-minded citizens rose to the call and offered parcels of land for a nominal or token price. In this way the city created three new parks: Sunrise Park on two acres from Frank Cook, Harrison Park on 1.8 acres from Duffy Reed, and the 3-acre Harry Barry Park from David, Warren, and Arlene Barry in memory of their parents Harry and Harriet Barry who died in an automobile accident in 1954.

> *The swimming pool at Harry Barry Park that was built in 1956 lasted until the City Pool was built in the late '80s. Parks and Rec brought in a building from the Hunt Camp and put restrooms in one end and a rec room in the other end. They had summer recreation programs then.* —Warren Barry (1998)

Harmon Park's 1935 round pool was filled in to install a playground, and a new pool was built. Parks and Rec worked with the Red Cross on water safety and swim lessons (twenty-five cents); Art Frantz directed the program. In 1956 Harmon Park acquired a demilitarized General Sherman tank and Jaycee Field received a merry-go-round from the Twentieth Century Club.

Communications expanded. During the war, communication systems became as widespread as travel. By 1946, Twin Falls boasted three radio stations. KTFI, which was licensed in 1928 and joined NBC in 1938, got most of its programming from national networks. Franklin Ver Cox, who worked at KTFI for ten years becoming its chief engineer, formed a new radio station. From Cox's KVMV (Voice of Magic Valley) booth on top of the stands behind home plate in Jaycee Field, Joe Clements broadcast the Cowboy baseball games.

> *I never saw a game in person that was as exciting as the ones I listened to over the radio . . . Who can forget the crack of the bat, followed by his voice ringing out those words, "It's a hit!" The hair on my head would stand up and I'd get goose pimples all over. Joe's genius made the Cowboys bigger than life.* —Dick Huizinga, Burley (2002)

KLIX of the ABC-affiliated Rocky Mountain Network was the third station to go on the air.

The first FM station was broadcast from KTFI in 1948, and for seven years it was "KTFI AM-FM." In that span of time, the first female announcer, Marge Van Amberg, made her debut on the air as did the first

Spanish-speaking announcer, Jesse Berain. The Magic Valley market did not take to FM, and KTFI ceased to broadcast FM in 1955. KTFI AM would change hands a few times and the studio would move to its present location at its transmitter site on U.S. Route 30 west of town. Radio Rondevoo would become Skateland in the 1970s.

Magic Valley's first television station went on the air at KLIX in 1954 and was owned and operated by the Southern Idaho Broadcasting and TV Company. But a Duopoly Law in 1965 would force KLIX Radio and KLIX TV to split, and KLIX TV would become KMVT, Channel 11. KLIX Radio would remain on Elizabeth Avenue until 1981 when the station would move to Kimberly. In 1987 KMVT TV would move and give the Elizabeth Avenue building to the Senior Center.

Cable Vision was initiated in 1958 by William L. Reiher who came to Twin Falls in 1931 with a few cents in his pocket and would leave $2 million to the College of Southern Idaho Foundation. Cable Vision changed owners and names several times. Finally, King Company would purchase it in the late 1970s, and the last name change would be made in 1983. King Videocable Company would become a multimillion dollar television, video, and audio service under its general manager from 1983 to 1989, Chris Talkington. With a newspaper background, Talkington would first work for Boise Radio and then as KMVT's news director before joining King. Chris would also serve on the city council from 1975 to 1982, act as mayor for one term, and would serve again from 1994 to 2006.

Civic Pride Was Evident

On 31 May 1948, five years after the death of I. B. Perrine, the Twin Falls-Jerome Intercounty Bridge was renamed the Perrine Memorial Bridge for the Father of Twin Falls. Probate Judge S. T. Hamilton was master of ceremonies, and the laudation was delivered by Joseph H. Seaver Sr. Perrine's daughter, Stella Perrine Haight, unveiled the monument with its plaque (situated by the stone wall at the Buzz Langdon Visitor Center). The first wreath was laid by Mrs. E. B. Williams who had managed the Perrine Hotel dining room for eleven years after it opened in 1905 while Mr. Williams managed the hotel. U.S. Route 93, which traverses the bridge, was completed in 1958.

A proud city and its government were upgraded.

> *Between 1948 and 1961, John E. Hayes completed designs, surveys, filings, and descriptions for more than forty subdivisions of Twin Falls and supervised the construction of many.* —Anna Hansen Hayes

Twin Falls voted for a city manager form of government in 1949 and replaced the 5-member city commission (since 1922) with a 7-member city council with one member chosen to be mayor. The seven members were elected on a non-partisan ballot for a term of four years; three were elected every two years to provide overlapping terms.

> *With a city manager, Twin Falls was the first city in Idaho to go to the 3-platoon system with firemen working 56 hours a week instead of the previous 84 hours under the 2-shift system.*
>
> —Bob K. Bopp, retired fire chief (2001)

The 1950 census showed that 17,544 people called Twin Falls home making it the fifth largest city in Idaho after Boise, Pocatello, Idaho Falls, and Nampa. With a population over fifteen thousand, "Twin Falls, City of the First Class" was declared by executive order of Gov. Lynn Jordan on 31 August 1951. The next year, the city council moved into a new City Hall on Second Avenue E; local architect Harald Gerber was one of the designers. Taxes were low; the state's first permanent sales tax was only 3 percent. Sportsmen found low fees for resident licenses: fishing, three dollars; fish and game, five dollars.

The League of Women Voters, which was organized in 1947, showed its civic pride. Their first project was to put a bond election on the ballot in the 1950s for a new sewage plant. The vote was 3–2 against rather than for, and the League's members were devastated.

> *The people figured a sewage disposal plant was a luxury!*
>
> —Helen Thorne, member (1999)

Their president was quoted in *The Times-News* as saying "We've just begun to fight." Another two decades of fighting by the League of Women Voters would pass before their project would become a reality, and not a luxury.

A new organization took pride in history. Articles of association for the Twin Falls County Historical Society were drawn up in 1957 and signed by Elizabeth (Mrs. Arthur) Peavy, Gus Kelker, Juneau Shinn, Earl Peck, and Helen (Mrs. Ledyard) Perrine; DeWitt R. Young was the first president. With dues at one dollar, membership rose to over two hundred.

> *We took tours all over Idaho in two or three school busses—east to a powwow in Pocatello, north to Soldier Mountain, Stanley, Salmon, west to mining towns and on the Oregon Trail—all over.*
>
> —Helen Porterfield, first secretary (1999)

The first contribution to the Historical Society, a 36-star American flag, was made by Pete Creed—the farmer whose gigantic pumpkins took the prize at the county fairs and whose suggestion to use landfill where Blue Lakes Boulevard crossed Rock Creek gave the town "Creed's Crossing." Contributions flooded in: Pete's buggies and wagons, Mr. Jones's farm machinery, furniture from closing stores, Miriam Breckenridge and her mother's wedding dress, Helen Perrine's and Mrs. Morgan Heap's Paris frocks that these wealthy ex-easterners ordered before Twin Falls had fine dress shops, and more.

In 1960 the Fair Board provided temporary space for the growing collection in one of its buildings at the fairgrounds, but a permanent storage place was necessary. Union School (at Curry Crossing) would close in 1968 and be deeded to the county. At this location the next year, the Historical Society would establish, maintain, and operate the Twin Falls County Historical Society Museum. The Society would be incorporated in 1987, and the Museum would become a Visitor Center in 2002.

UNION SCHOOL

Hispanic cultural pride was also evident. When farm labor shortages continued during the 1950s, Amalgamated Sugar Company and the Employment Security Agency (ESA) actively recruited workers from other states. Mexican-American families, mostly from southern Texas, migrated to fill seasonal agricultural jobs, and many settled in the Magic Valley where working conditions were harsh. One migrant worker who was born in Monterey, Mexico, and grew up in Texas brought his wife and twelve children to the Twin Falls Migrant Labor Camp in 1950. Jorge Galvan worked in the beet, onion, and potato fields of Stan Detweiler, George Coiner, and Bud Morgan. "George" soon became crew leader and paymaster. He brought his crews from Texas in a canvas-covered truck. One Texan, nineteen-year-old Jesse Berain, lived in a gunny sack in City Park until George's wife Maria took him in.

> *The government paid him* [Galvan] *one dollar per person, and he brought a lot of workers!* —Rosa Hernandez Pais, granddaughter (2000)

On 1 June 1957 the ESA and the Twin Falls Chamber of Commerce sponsored a fiesta. Jesse Berain, then a young crew leader, organized the program and served as master of ceremonies for a day of music, dance, and speeches on Main Avenue in front of the Bank and Trust Building. Baseball games were played in Harmon Park between teams from the Twin Falls, Buhl, Rupert, Burley, and Nyssa, Oregon, labor camps.

> *Our program is intended to promote good relations between migrant laborers and residents, and this fiesta will show that the workers are more than just laborers on our farms.*
>
> —Don Larsen, public relations representative for the ESA

Twin Falls Mexican-Americans took the ESA's festival idea and made the occasion their own annual *Cinco de Mayo* celebration involving the entire valley. In 1992 after moving to Caldwell, Jesse Berain would run for the Idaho legislature and beat an Anglo incumbent by 244 votes to become Idaho's first Hispanic legislator.

The Spheres of Music and Art Widened

Helen (Mrs. Charles) Allen organized the Music Club in 1951 to sponsor music and culture in the community. This club was the impetus for the formation of several local performing groups: the Community Choir (progenitor of the CSI Chorale) which presented the *Messiah* every Christmas, the Men's Chorus, and local self-productions such as *Carmen*. The Music Club treated Twin Falls citizens to concerts such as the Utah Symphony and the Boise Opera Company's production of *Madam Butterfly*. They chartered busses to Boise to take in a Van Cliburn concert, and others. As a sideline the first music scholarship was awarded by the Music Club in 1957. But after the 1965 founding of the College of Southern Idaho, Music Club functions and fund-raisers for music scholarships would be sponsored by the college.

> *The community didn't need the Music Club any more to promote culture through local groups, and our emphasis turned toward kids. We sponsor annually a festival to audition solo student musicians and award $2,000 or more in scholarships for graduating seniors and for summer music camp for younger students.*
>
> —Patty Hadley, former Music Club president (2002)

City Park's summer band concerts got a new director in 1955 when Del Slaughter and his wife Julienne, both music teachers, came to Twin Falls. Music in Twin Falls would get better when Del also taught band and orchestra at the high school and directed the Twin Falls Civic Symphony while Julienne introduced the Suzuki method of learning to play musical instruments.

> *He* [Del] *gave himself to the musical community.*
>
> —Burt Huish, new resident in 1965

A musical theater group became the Dilettantes in 1959. For many years the Presbyterian Church had a Couples Club which met monthly for a dinner and program with four couples hosting. One program, a shadow production of *The Mikado* lip-synced to the music, was received with so much enthusiasm that "Twin Falls's desire for something musical was obvious." Marty Mead and Vern Hedner's idea of a musical theater group gave birth to the Dilettantes. With Bert Sweet directing, Roger Vincent as "Billy Bigelow," and Marty Mead as "Julie Jordan," the Dilettantes presented *Carousel* to the public on the cramped stage of the (original) O'Leary Junior

High School auditorium. The next year's production of the musical was presented in Filer's auditorium with its roomier stage.

> *It was ridiculous that Twin Falls didn't have a decent auditorium.*
>
> —Marty Mead

So the Dilettantes formed the Civic Auditorium Association with Hank Wills as its president. The Dilettantes took $2,000 from its shows' profits, borrowed $8,000, and kicked off the fund-raising drive in 1960. One fund-raiser was the Aqua Ballet which brought its own swimming pool to Harmon Park. The Dilettantes would hire a full-time, professional fund-raiser in 1964, and fourteen hundred subscribers would pledge $548,400 (the largest private money donation to date). The Gala Opening of the Civic Auditorium-Fine Arts Building on the new CSI campus would be held on 13 November 1968. The next year, the Dilettantes would present *My Fair Lady*, their first production in that spacious auditorium.

The orchestra for the Dilettantes' production of *Carousel* in 1959 became the Twin Falls Civic Symphony in 1960, both directed by Richard Smith. The Symphony featured soloists—regional artists from Southern Idaho, Boise, Salt Lake City—in two concerts a year. With completion of the new auditorium at CSI, the Symphony would come under the auspices of the college, which would provide financing and credit. The Symphony would then bring to Twin Falls such famous guest performers as Eugene Fodor, the Romeros, Jose Greco, and the Kingston Trio.

> *So many musicians came from outside Twin Falls to play in the orchestra that the name was changed to Magic Valley Civic Symphony.*
>
> —Ted Hadley, music director and conductor (2002)

The Art Guild of Magic Valley was founded in 1956. The purpose of the Guild was to advance the participation and interest in the Arts throughout the Magic Valley. This non-profit organization would support schools and fund scholarships for artists. In 1959 the Guild began the annual Art in the Park show in City Park. This show and sale would grow to feature fine arts, original crafts, food, entertainment, demonstrations, a junior gallery, and cash awards. This July event would be renamed Summer Fine Arts Festival in 2002.

The Guild encourages artists to create in a wide variety of visual media by providing art festivals and monthly meetings for showing ideas and works of art. —Ingrid Strope, past president (2002)

In the fifteen years following the end of World War II, the citizens of Twin Falls demonstrated a talent for advancing the signs of civilization that Clarence Bisbee's 1906 postcards advertised as they continued in the tradition of Grace Seaver's "jolliest, most enthusiastic people you ever saw."

Seen at TWIN FALLS COUNTY HISTORICAL SOCIETY MUSEUM

Chapter 14

Fifteen Boom Years Led into the 1960s

With the end of World War II came the end of Twin Falls's struggling "Pioneer Era." War veterans and defense plant workers returned to their old jobs, to their family businesses, to start new jobs and businesses. As the town grew and offered more amenities, it continued to attract mobile Americans from around the country looking for a new home. Here they found a friendly and progressive city in which to live and work. Together the returnees, newcomers, pioneers and other homefront folks created the "Post–War Boom Era" and restored Twin Falls to the prosperous and vibrant town that I. B. Perrine created half a century before.

The Post–War Boom Saw "New Kids on the Block"

South Dakota native Ernie "E. J." Wills with sons Bob and Hank, both veterans of WWII, opened Wills Motors in 1946 on Shoshone Street W. The company went from the Nash make of cars to Jeep in 1960 and switched to Toyota in 1965.

A new Riser-Cain store next to the Orpheum Theater began selling Frigidaire appliances in 1946. After Elvis Cain became sole owner, he renamed the store Cain's and took on two partners. In 1963 Cain's moved into the 1909 Consolidated Wagon Company Building after it was vacated by Detweiler Brothers and expanded to a full service home furnishing store. Cain took on another partner in 1967: outdoorsman Les Hazen who started the *vignette* (small room) type of merchandising display. Hazen's *vignette* was the first to appear in a popular-priced furniture store in Idaho (and perhaps in the country) and would come to be used in all such furniture stores.

Christina Petersen gave up her job at the Park Hotel in 1946 and struck out on her own making leather jackets and repairs while raising four children. After making her first leather coat and fringed shirt for Slim Pickens, a popular western movies star, Christina made many more items of apparel for him. This enterprise led to her "Chris Line Originals" and to her being named Idaho Mother of the Year in 1967. Her son Emery and his wife Ruby would buy Chris's popular westernwear business in 1973.

In 1947, after his service in the Air Force as pilot and flight instructor, Rudy Ashenbrener purchased Price Hardware. From Nampa, Idaho, Rudy and his wife Marjorie settled in Twin Falls where Ashenbrener became an anchor of the community. Starting in the fall of 1981, Rudy's son Tom would stage annual Dutch Oven Cookoffs in front of the store at 147 Main Street W. The donations his customers gave for sampling the foods would go to such local charities as People for Pets.

Downtown is just a place that feels like home.

—Tom Ashenbrener (1990)

Rudy would continue his military career as a commander in the Air Reserves and finally retire as a colonel. In 1991 Tom would purchase the business, which he would claim to be "the oldest retail business in Twin Falls" since it had evolved from the hardware store that Roy W. Gager opened in 1904. November 2000 would commemorate the death of an outstanding Twin Falls citizen; Rudy Ashenbrener was eighty-three.

Ray Lytle came to Twin Falls from Nebraska after learning the art of glass blowing in New York City on the GI Bill. Ray took a job with Cosgriff Sign Company, was laid off, and started his own sign company in 1948. Lytle's first shop was in the back of a radiator shop on Second Avenue N. His business grew, and he would move it several times before 1975 when he would take the (present) location at 1925 Kimberly Road. Ray would retire in 1982 and his son Rex would run the business. Rex would donate the design work for many civic projects such as the attractive signs leading to the Historic Rock Creek Station and Stricker Homesite south of Hansen.

Glass blowing is not computerized. It is still the art of the glass blower.
—Rex Lytle (1999)

Nebraskan Leonard C. Scott and son Jack left their jobs with Detweiler Brothers in 1949 to start their own Scott's Refrigeration business and bought Detweiler's refrigeration department. Jack and his two younger brothers then served in the Korean Conflict, returning home in the late 1950s. Jack Scott patented his design for an integrated refrigeration system that would have significant impact on the refrigeration and air-conditioning industry nationwide. Scott's 1964 subsidiary, Polar Manufacturing, built Jack's customized integrated systems.

Kay Kawamoto came back to Twin Falls and worked for Gus Kelker in his photo shop. We met the Kawamotos at Hunt Camp where they were interned during World War II. When the war ended, the family returned to Portland to the strawberry farm they had to abandon in 1942. They had stored everything on rented property, and when they returned, almost everything was gone. "It was very hard to start over." The Twin Falls community had long known its Japanese pioneers—the Kotos, the Gikius—but Kay was from the misnomered "concentration camp" and he had to overcome prejudice.

I got to know a lot of people [at Gus Kelker's] *and worked hard to promote good will.*
—Kay Kawamoto

Kay's brother George joined him in 1952, and with Chinese cooks hired from San Francisco, they opened Twin Falls's first Chinese restaurant, the Rice Bowl, at East Five Points. This restaurant burned down in 1955, and the Kawamotos opened a second Rice Bowl on Addison Avenue W. When they got a license to serve liquor by the glass, they changed the name to Kay's Supper Club, which one or the other brother would run until the 1970s.

Earl Faulkner bought the Paris Department Store in 1952 after returning from service in Japan during World War II. Earl and his wife Hazel would run the Paris at 124 Main Avenue N for thirty-eight years. They knew their customers so well that if a man came in for a present for his wife, Earl or

Hazel would pick it out for him. Faulkner based his success on such rules as "The customer always comes first in business as in life," "Find a way to give back to the community," and "Be honest and treat your customers right."

Walgreen's pulled out of town (to return in 2002) leaving the Baugh Building's store empty at the corner of Main and Shoshone N. In 1954 Leonard Emerson, pharmacist and veteran of the U.S. Navy, opened his City Drug in that space.

> *My partner left me after three weeks. After that my wife and I and three girls ran the store every day for thirty years. Two doctors said I couldn't survive it. They're both gone; I'm still here.*
>
> —Leonard Emerson (age ninety-two, 2003)

Eight partners started Idaho Frozen Foods in 1955 to produce the RUS-ETTES brand of frozen shredded hash browns using only Idaho Russet potatoes. In 1961 they entered the frozen french fry business, and in 1966 they sold the company to Consolidated Foods Corporation (Sarah Lee).

Fidelity National Bank (established in 1935) installed Twin Falls's first drive-in facility in 1955 on Third Avenue E off Shoshone. Fidelity bought Perrine's First National Bank of Twin Falls (on the corner of Main and Shoshone E, now Key Bank) and also installed the first time-and-temperature sign in the county in 1959.

Leo and Bob Soran acquired the Depot Grill in 1959. We saw the Mays family convert Deigart's Depot Service and Texaco Station, in the original Benoit's bottling building, into the Depot Grill in 1935, and it changed hands again in 1942. The Soran brothers made sixteen structural changes that included the Caboose Room, the first smorgasbord in Twin Falls. The Sorans added a catering service in 1963. They would cater to groups of from four people to five thousand people at Lamb-Weston's cafeteria, the Magic Valley Speedway, and the Turf Club.

The Turf Club was built in 1946 for gambling and drinking before Idaho outlawed slot machines and before Twin Falls banned liquor by the drink—

for a time. In 1949 the Turf became a supper club and night club; the clientele came from nearby Frontier Field where the Frontier Riding Club held horse races. The Sorans purchased the spacious Turf Club in 1969, and it became a popular special events and meetings place. Leo would buy out Bob's interest in 1974, and his sons Steve and Tim would join the family business.

In 1962 Dean and Jim Vickers purchased Max's Harness Shop on Third Avenue S at Shoshone and renamed it Vickers Saddlery, and later, Vickers Western Store. The building, which dated back to the 1920s, had never been used for anything other than a harness or western shop and would have only three owners in its eighty-some years.

> *We know of no other western store in the Northwest that is still being run by its original owners for a longer continuous period of time.*
>
> —Jim Vickers (2002)

Added to the list of newcomer businesses in Twin Falls following the War were Fox Floral and Roper's Clothing Company in 1949, Benno's Fine Jewelry in 1960, the second Perrine Barber Shop in 1961, and Moore Signs in 1963.

> *The Beatles' hair style lost us a bundle of money. My wife even had to go back to work.* —Keith Burgess, Perrine Barber Shop (2001)

In 1963 Dan Obenchain bought Twin Falls's first insurance agency, the one that Sprague and Robertson began in a tent in 1904 and later named the Irrigated Lands Company. In 1930 Robertson's son John became its proprietor, and he formed a partnership with John Whitsell. After the death of Whitsell, Obenchain bought that agency. So Obenchain Insurance Company would claim to be "the oldest business in Twin Falls."

The first mall, the Lynwood Shopping Center at Blue Lakes Boulevard and Filer Avenue in the early 1960s, and the first multiplex theater at Kimberly and Eastland Roads later that decade, were found on the "outskirts" of the growing town. In 1966, three years after Twin Falls celebrated the Idaho Territorial Centennial, travel and tourism were enhanced by a new $1.2 million Hansen Bridge that replaced the forty-seven-year-old suspension bridge, the highest in its day.

Some Stickers Stuck for Half to Three Quarters of a Century

When Charles and Howard Allen returned from military service in 1946, they purchased from their mother the business their father started in 1910. While Charles tended the store, Howard went to watch-making school in Denver and returned to the family business in 1947. The Allen brothers' Sterling Jewelry Store would continue to serve the community for another forty-one years.

> *Sterling Jewelry Company gave the "Most Valuable Player Award" each year . . . a 19-jewel Hamilton watch* [at the end of every Cowboys baseball season]. —Virginia Ricketts, historian (1998)

~

A. M. Sande added many facets to his Twin Falls Feed and Ice Company before he died in 1954. After World War II, Sande's mechanical refrigeration made tons of ice in a single day to pack box cars of local fruit for shipment east. As truck transport replaced rail freight, Sande sold ice for "reefer" (refrigerator) trucks. Sande added large locker rooms for cold storage and serviced Swift and Company, Bertie's Poultry Company, Blue Lakes Trout Company, Utah Wholesale Grocery, the USDA (Department of Agriculture) with its surplus items for the school hot lunch program, and smaller customers before the arrival of home freezers. From retail stores Sande sold countless tons of livestock feed, thousands of baby chicks, plus garden supplies and bedding plants. After Sande's death, his three nephews would run the family business until 1971. The last employee, Ted Samples, would close its doors in 1984 after seventy-seven years of business.

> *Late at night* [the old building] *moaned in agony under the pressure of cold winter winds. . . When I locked the door for the last time on that October morning . . . there were tears in my eyes as I stepped into the street and gazed up at her aging façade. The windows were boarded over. There were cracks in her bricks. But for her historic past, there was no reason for apology.* —Ted Samples

On Memorial Day 1989, A. M. Sande's seventy-three-year-old Twin Falls Feed and Ice Building on Shoshone Street and Fifth Avenue S would go up in flames, cause unknown.

WWII veteran Tom Koto moved back to Twin Falls in 1958. In the depression we saw Tom's parents close their restaurant after twenty-three years in Twin Falls and run another restaurant in Shoshone. When young Tom got out of the army, he took his new bride Matsuye, "the Salem girl from Hunt Camp," home to Shoshone. In Twin Falls Tom, his wife, and his brother Ernest opened the second generation Koto's Café at 147 Shoshone N (recently A'Roma), which they would operate for twenty years.

When peacetime returned and government defense contracts expired, the Detweiler Brothers moved into the Consolidated Wagon Company Building. (Remodeling included installing a forty-horse-power electric motor to operate the original 8-by-12-foot cargo elevator still in use, which was operated by pulling a rope on a large capstan to position the elevator on one of three floors.) Detweiler Brothers entered into the field of construction of telephone and power lines in 1950 and were licensed in ten states. They contracted for work with the Atomic Energy Commission, and their work at the new Hanford, Washington, and Arco, Idaho, sites was highly classified: their crews helped assemble the first equipment for testing the atomic submarine and for the first atomic plant to generate electricity (for Arco).

As the contracting business took more of their time, the Detweilers divested their interests. They sold their refrigeration division to Scott's Refrigeration, their heating department to Warberg Brothers, their plumbing department to Vern Thomas, and their appliance interests to The Music Center. Claude Detweiler was killed on a business trip in 1957, and George continued alone to make a final move to the Ostrander Lumber Company Building at 726 Shoshone Street W. George Detweiler would retire in 1978 and close the doors on a pioneer family firm that gave this valley fifty-seven years of experience which included the fields of engineering and mechanical contracting. The Detweiler expertise was extended throughout this country in times of both war and peace.

At least 90% of the plumbing, heating, sheet metal, and electrical firms in Twin Falls got their initial training at Detweiler Brothers.

—Donna Scott, author-editor (1990)

Jenny Stewart let a contract in 1947 to two men to manage her Rogerson Restaurant. Ben Mottern and Ted Smith ran a "scratch" restaurant: all food was prepared on the premises and the chefs cut their own chops, roasts, ground their own hamburger, etcetera. The Rogerson specialty was 8-inch oatmeal cookies. As many as fourteen waitresses, earning $.60 an hour plus tips, served lunch at $1.00 and dinner at $1.75 including beverage and dessert. A waitress competition was held in Twin Falls in the mid-1950s, and the Rogerson waitresses won the first three places in the contest. Ben and Ted sponsored a little league team, the Rogerson Restaurant Giants, which was almost unbeaten in its nine-year lifetime.

Nationally, the Rogerson Restaurant received recognition from . . . Duncan Hines . . . an excellent rating.

—Ben and Jim Mottern and Ted Smith (1990)

The 1908 Rogerson Hotel remained with the Hoops Family until the early 1970s. Jenny sold her Park Hotel (begun in 1907 as a hospital) in 1960 to the city to be razed to make way for the new U. S. Post Office Building the following year. The Hoops family was in business in Twin Falls for roughly sixty years.

After nineteen years in business, Santa Bilbao had her boardinghouse completely paid for. But this exceptional woman fell ill, and in 1949 she died at the age of sixty-one.

With Santa's death went the end of an era. The decline in the need for Basque boardinghouses [occurred when] *large sheep ranchers such as Breckenridge and Guerry sold their operations . . .*

—Rosa Sofia, Isabel Mendiola, and Ruth Glenn (1990)

Ernest Bengochea purchased the boardinghouse in 1954. In 1975 Bengochea would lease the house—for forty-five years a *posada*—to the Alcohol Rehabilitation Center.

Twin Falls lost another pioneer on 3 June 1954 with the death of Clarence Bisbee. This legendary photographer of Twin Falls excelled in photography of buildings, crowds, and landscapes from 1906 to 1939. Flowers, Amos, Helm, Wheeling, Kelker, and other photographers set up businesses in Twin Falls at better locations than Bisbee's; some sold photographic equipment, which Bisbee did not; and some did portraiture, which Bisbee did not.

> *One photographer, C. E. Jacoby, got the contract to photograph the high school seniors and juniors for their yearbooks.* —Fred Sanger

Bisbee simply did not go with the popular trends in the photography business. He invested all he had in real property, and Clarence Bisbee died broke after forty-eight years behind the camera.

Other Pioneer Businesses Would Stick for the Town's Centennial

Brizee Metal Works installed the first water-cooled air conditioner in a residence in 1954. We saw Harry Brizee install the first residential oil furnace in 1937. Oil furnaces generally replaced coal furnaces after World War II; the arrival of natural gas to Twin Falls in 1957 all but eliminated coal as heating fuel. Leland Brizee introduced the first electric furnace, then heat pumps, and changed the name of the family business—which then included Leland's son Richard—to Brizee Heating and Air Conditioning Company. Leland would pass away in 1978 after fifty-nine years in the business, and Richard would take over to provide more service for the more complex systems. In 1982 third-generation Daniel would join the business: "the oldest company under one family ownership and at one location (since 1919), and one of the oldest Lennox dealers in the Western United States" . . . and it would still be going in 2004 after ninety-five years.

Three of Otto Florence Sr.'s sons returned from World War II armed service in 1945. In the depression Otto Sr. had purchased one-third interest in the Independent Meat Company, and by 1940 he was half owner. Together his three sons bought the remaining interest in the company.

> *By then all the meat markets had been closed and a new era as a slaughterer, meat processor, and wholesale distributor had begun.*
>
> —Otto Florence Jr.

The Florences made major expansions of the business and additions to the plant on 3700 N. Otto Sr. was inducted into the first Southern Idaho Livestock Hall of Fame in 1960, Otto Jr. was so honored in 1968, Ted would be in 1978, and third generation Patrick would be inducted in 2003. Since the 1930s, four generations of Florences would be investors in the ninety-four-year-old company come 2004.

Charles "Cap" Krengel made his machine shop a separate business from the hardware store in 1952 and put it in a new metal building at 211–227 Third Avenue S (since demolished). Then Cap's prodigiously inventive mind took a surprising turn to food.

> *In 1955 a gourmet bar with imported cheese, ham, rattlesnake meat, alligator soup, and 56 kinds of hard candy was added.*
>
> —Jean Cilek and Matt Thomas (1990)

Cap's gourmet shop was such a success that it received national attention in trade magazines. In 1957, the store's fiftieth anniversary, Krengel was named Hardware Dealer of the Year for the Intermountain Region. Cap sold his store to Joe Cilek in 1962 and stayed on as advisor until his death in 1966. From 1994, Jerry Fisher and Art Cristler would own and operate Krengel's True Value Hardware (now at 628 Main Avenue S), which would have a ninety-seven-year history in 2004.

Larry Clos hired Ed Purves right out of the army in 1945. We last saw Larry in 1915 dispensing text books to students from his Clos Book Store, which he had founded three years earlier. Purves became Clos's partner in 1946. After Clos's death in 1948 and his wife Harriet's death in 1959, Ed Purves became sole owner and manager.

> *Probably the single most remembered item about our store in the '50s and '60s was the large BOOK sign that opened and closed at regular intervals.*
>
> —Betty Purves (1990)

When schools started selling their own books and more book stores set up business in Twin Falls, the Clos store became more office-oriented. In 1965 Purves expanded his store and moved to its (present) location at 150 Main Avenue S. Ed and his wife Jane would retire in 1976 and their son Jim would purchase the store. Jim and Betty Purves would eliminate the book department, and in 1980 the store would become the Clos Office Supply, which would celebrate ninety-two years of business in 2004.

Gary Babbel, third generation in Babbel's Dry Cleaners business, would celebrate eighty-three years of his family's business in 2004. Hudson's Shoes would discontinue its Main Avenue Store, retaining its Lynwood store, in 2002, and in 2004 would mark seventy-three years in business. The 1989 First Federal Savings Bank of Twin Falls, which began in 1916 as the Twin Falls Building and Loan Association, would celebrate eighty-eight years in 2004.

> *In 1919 Claude Brown opened the Claude Brown Music Company with musical instruments of all kinds and sizes.*
>
> —Doug Brown, grandson (2000)

Later, Claude Brown added appliances to his music store, and just before World War II he added furniture; his son Claude Jr. managed the drapery department. Pianos and organs were the main stock in Brown's music store at 143 Main E (which is still known as the Claude Brown Music Company Building). When Claude Jr.'s sons Karl, Doug, and Mark returned from military service after the War, they expanded the furniture department and eventually dropped the appliances. The Browns would buy the old J. C. Penney Building at 202 Main Avenue S in 1990 and discontinue their music line. A fourth generation of Browns would continue to feature fine furniture and floor coverings as well as a carpet cleaning service. The Browns would celebrate eighty-five years of a family business in 2004 in a town celebrating its own one hundred years of serving more than its agricultural community.

A Time to Rededicate

After the opening of the new Robert Stuart Junior High School in 1963, education got another boost. The voters of Twin Falls and Jerome Counties created a college taxing district, and the Idaho State Board of Regents appointed five members to a board of trustees to administer a two-year College of Southern Idaho. CSI opened in 1965 with night classes at Twin Falls High School; the college moved to its campus with its bell tower three years later. A Fine Arts Auditorium for concerts, plays, and forums was built in 1968 with private donations of almost $550,000 raised by the Dilettantes' Civic Auditorium Association and $10,000 from the Twentieth Century Club.

> *. . . the establishment of a suitable Fine Arts Building for educational and theatrical purposes for the full use and benefit of all bonafide civic, political, and cultural groups of Southcentral Idaho.*
>
> —Contract between CSI and the Civic Auditorium Association

The Twin Falls Municipal Golf Course became an 18-hole course in the 1960s. (The swales of the Oregon Trail are still seen running through the fairway on hole No. 9.)

First Lady "Lady Bird" Johnson's national campaign to Clean Up America got underway in the late 1960s, and the Twentieth Century Club's national office gave awards of $2,500 for the best projects. The local club's president, Mrs. D. A. Jackson, proposed the project of cleaning up Rock Creek north of Addison Avenue—then being used as a dump—and turning it into a park. The club was awarded the $2,500 and the members went to work in 1969 with the help of Don Zuck, chairman of the Board of County Parks (established in 1965); Ed Woods, executive director of County Parks and Solid Waste, with Bob Maxwell, director of County Parks (now superintendent of City Parks); and Darrell Heider, director of Solid Waste.

With the assistance of the Air National Guard's helicopter, Heider removed sixty-nine junked cars to the Filer dump to be crushed. When that proved too slow, the crusher was brought to Rock Creek for another one hundred cars. Zuck installed drain pipes in the county land along the creek, which was low and swampy, and brought in tons of fill. Grass would not grow—too alkaline—and ninety-two tons of gypsum were hauled in from Pocatello to start a lawn. The Twin Falls Lions Club helped to build the shelters. After a flood of Rock Creek in the 1970s, land on the north side of the creek would be purchased from the Canal Company, bulldozed and leveled, and a bridge would be installed.

> *That 70-foot bridge is two flatcars from the Union Pacific Railroad in Pocatello. The railings are the sprinkler-system pipe from O'Leary Junior High.* —Darrell Heider (2002)

A Time to Re-evaluate

Downtown business owners and managers re-evaluated what they saw happening in their downtown (and other parts of the country) in the mid-1960s and they didn't like it.

> *There were six bars and three or four brothels within two blocks of the Twin Falls Bank and Trust Building where we had our jewelry store. The town was going to the dogs. Something had to be done.*
>
> —Howard Allen

Commercial strips were pulling business away from downtown areas and they didn't want that to happen to Twin Falls. A group including Rudy Ashenbrener, Howard Allen, Voy Hudson, John Roper, Curtis T. Eaton, Earl Faulkner, David Mead, Joe Cilek, and others started a movement dedicated to bolstering Twin Falls downtown against the incoming wave of chain retailing.

> *We want to put life back into downtown. We want to put the heart back into the city.* —1960s businessmen

The Idaho legislature passed the Idaho Urban Renewal Act in May 1965 that allowed each town to create an Urban Renewal Agency (URA), an independent public body. Twin Falls did just that in July. The City Council appointed a 5-member administrative board with Voy Hudson as chairman, and the URA set to work on a general plan for an improvement program. After three years of study regarding off-street parking, clearance and development of land occupied by obsolete structures, and construction of a modern mall, they came up with a plan for a central business district urban renewal project.

For funding, the URA applied for a grant from the Federal Department of Housing and Urban Development (HUD) which earmarked $1.4 million for the project. But matching funds of $600,000 had to be obtained and the project had to be approved by the citizens of Twin Falls before the grant would be funded. Pledges of $390,000 were obtained from the city, and the rest would still have to be raised. For this purpose the citizens' group asked the City Council to create and administer a Local Improvement District (LID) to include three blocks on both sides of Main Avenue between Second Streets N and W and Third Streets S and E, which was to become the "pedestrian mall." The property owners in the LID were assessed to pay for the fifteen-year bond, plus there would be other pledged revenues for a total of $610,000. The project was oversubscribed (!). Approval came from the public in an open hearing, the City Council accepted the project, and HUD approved the funding in July 1968.

> *Twin Falls's urban renewal project was the first in the Northwest to be closed out* [completed] *by HUD.*
>
> —Dave McAlindin, Director URA (2002)

John Robertson sold his family's landmark Perrine Hotel that was built sixty-three years earlier to accommodate the many prospective investors and settlers that came to look over the new town in Idaho (still being confused with Iowa). The hotel was razed and the new owners built the Bank of Idaho Building (now Magic Valley Bank) on that corner of Main and Shoshone W.

> *Sadly, Twin Falls has lost one of the finest and the grandest of its hotels, the Perrine—outpost of civilization, source of beds and bath, home cooking, a court yard, even a conservatory.*
>
> —Patricia Wright, architect (1979)

Twin Falls's last remaining luxury hotel, the Rogerson, which had a kitchen fire in 1965 that leveled its third floor, became Rogerson Mall; the Rogerson Motel Inn was added at the rear on Second Avenue E. Proud old Main Avenue store fronts, many with ornate brickwork, got modern façades; the I. D. and the Rogerson were entirely hidden under their new exteriors. After the 3-story Booth Building was reduced to one and a half stories, Robert Crowley relegated his old-fashioned soda fountain to the rear of the store, carpeted the enlarged main floor, and installed a false ceiling to conceal the original decorative tin.

They put a backhoe on top of the Booth Building and took off the top stories. —Howard Allen

Main Avenue was torn up to produce wide sidewalks and "parking pods" to alternate with trees and flower beds where none had existed before. When finished, the overall impression would be of a modern, yet leisurely, shopping experience as in the "good old days" when people went downtown to meet other people and to sit and visit. But the denuded, muddy/dusty alleys and streets were all too reminiscent of Twin Falls's earliest days before paving when customers had to wipe their feet and store owners swept their floors and dusted their cases hourly.

It was a mess, because customers couldn't reach the businesses conveniently. —Les Hazen (1999)

With streets torn up in the summer of 1970, six horseshoe pits were set up—one at each end of three blocks—and each block had four teams that played at noon. Even bankers loosened their collars and came out in their shiny shoes to play. Once a week, after 5 P.M., the teams played for block winners. —David Mead, retired banker (2000)

The Rogerson Mall acquired Sterling Jewelry as a tenant in 1970; Babbel's Dry Cleaners was moved to 228 Shoshone E. In all, thirty-four businesses in the LID were aided in relocation and twenty-six sub-standard structures were demolished in the urban renewal project.

Downtown Twin Falls, shining like a new penny, had its Grand Opening in November 1970. The extensive urban renewal work surrounding the mall would be completed early in 1971: landscaping, improvements to downtown alleys, sidewalks, and parking lots, and to streets, giving them storm sewers and buried utilities.

The decade of the '60s ended on a tragic note when Twin Falls lost its first, and only, fireman in the line of duty. A fire at the Lynwood Shopping Center on 29 March 1969 trapped a twenty-one-year-old rookie in the basement of the Penny Wise Drug Store. Roy L. Parker died of smoke inhalation and carbon monoxide poisoning leaving a wife and two-year-old daughter.

Chapter 15

Decades of the '70s and '80s

Lars P. Larsen was one of the citizens meeting that first train when it arrived [on 7 August 1905]. . . . *Lars P. Larsen was one of three passengers on the last train out* [on 4 January 1970]. —Gus Kelker

The Union Pacific passenger depot was hauled away to Nat-Soo-Pah in 1972.

The Era of Mass Transportation Ended

The federally-funded Interstate 84 across Southern Idaho opened in 1974 to accommodate mobile America's love affair with the automobile. Like a magnet only three miles north of Twin Falls, Interstate 84 was bound to draw development in that direction and away from Twin Falls's southern arteries of road and rail. Along U.S. Route 30 (the Old Oregon Trail Highway, which the railroad parallels from Heyburn to Bliss) small farming communities would feel a double whammy as traffic and business dried up.

Twin Falls felt the existence of Interstate 84 immediately. More tourists arrived to enjoy Snake River boat tours and whitewater raft trips run by Don Mays and Olin Gardner, each licensed outfitters. Golfers arrived to try out a new 9-hole golf course opened at the Canyon Springs Country Club. Evel Knievel arrived to attempt to jump the Snake River Canyon on his rocket-powered motorcycle; he failed.

The multitudes of people that came to Twin Falls to live it up . . . left our parks and scenic areas a garbage dump. There were assaults . . . thefts, destruction of property, many drug-related arrests . . . and financial loss to many of our citizens.

—James R. Munn, Twin Falls County sheriff, retired (1999)

On September 8, 1974, Twin Falls was given the world's attention, but its innocence was taken away forever.

—*The Times-News*, 29 August 1999, 25th anniversary of "The Jump"

Construction of the new $9.7 million Perrine Bridge, on U.S. Route 93 that connects Twin Falls with the Interstate, was completed in 1976 amid celebrations of our country's Bicentennial. The Chambers of Commerce of Twin Falls and Jerome held the dedication ceremony on 31 July. Speakers were the mayors of both towns, the president of Allied Steel, and the contractor Farnham Jarrard. Eleven members of the Perrine family attended. Dan Obenchain was chairman of the fun and games: bicycle and foot races across the new bridge and a golf ball driving contest.

Historical Update: At that time the procedure of the Idaho Transportation Department was to assign numbers to bridges rather than names, and Twin Falls's new bridge got the number 17580. That was corrected in 2000 when a law was passed to reattach the chosen name of Perrine to the landmark.

The largest section of the old Perrine Bridge now spans the Salmon River above Clayton. . . . Some of the girders were re-used in the construction of hangars at the Twin Falls airport.

—Ray and Shirley Harris, Harris Tours (2002)

In response to the increased tourism fostered by the new Interstates, the Idaho legislature passed the Recreation and Tourism Act in 1983 that created the Idaho Travel Council and the hotel/motel head tax to fund it. To promote tourism the Twin Falls Chamber of Commerce (TFCC) formed a Western Days Committee the next year, and "Western Days" became an annual community event and tourist attraction. Through a joint financial effort of the TFCC and the Rotary Club, the Buzz Langdon Visitor Center opened in 1989 near the southwest end of the Perrine Bridge. The "VC" was named in honor of the former TFCC executive director who was instrumental in having it built and whose untimely death from cancer occurred before it opened.

BUZZ LANGDON VISITOR CENTER

The two questions that tourists ask most often at the Buzz Langdon Visitor Center are "Where is Shoshone Falls?" and "Where did Evel Knievel jump?"

—Kent Just, executive director,
Twin Falls Area Chamber of Commerce (2002)

Environment and Pollution Became Buzz Words

Increased cross-country motoring in the 1970s served to expose millions of Americans to what wonders were to be found in their land and what resources were being lost to rapid development and exploitation. Following up the Wilderness Act of 1964, Pres. Richard Nixon signed the Clean Water Act of 1972 and the Endangered Species Act of 1973. Idaho citizens gained Three Island State Park in 1971, the 750,000 acre Sawtooth National Recreation Area in 1972, and Malad Gorge State Park in 1979. Gov. Cecil Andrus resigned his position in 1977 to become Pres. Jimmy Carter's Secretary of the Interior, which oversees the BLM (Bureau of Land Management) and the NPS (National Park Service). The River of No Return Wilderness was established in 1980 by the Central Idaho Wilderness Act which was guided through Congress by Idaho Senator Frank Church; Andrus returned to Idaho in 1982 to be elected governor again. In 1984 Congress honored the senator by adding his name to the region making it the Frank Church River of No Return Wilderness. Four years later, the City of Rocks National Reserve was established.

In preparation for the nation's 200th birthday, the BLM launched in 1968 the national Johnny Horizon Day campaign to clean up roadside litter, then officially ended the program prematurely in 1972. To Darrell Heider this was too good a program to terminate. Heider, director of Twin Falls County Solid Waste, kept the program alive by recruiting hundreds of volunteers every year to clean up the county's roadsides for one day in May. Twin Falls County and the Twin Falls Lions Club sponsored the local annual Johnny Horizon Day. In 2001 Darrell Heider would be chosen Western Days' Pioneer of the Year.

> *Emphasis in the 1970s is on a cleaner environment, and pollution of streams and rivers is beginning to draw some long overdue action.*
>
> —Bonnie Baird Jones, *The Times-News* staff

Unfamiliar words such as environment, ecology, pollution, and zoning took their places in ordinary Twin Falls conversation, and then conversation turned into action. Smoke from the sugar factory chimney was criticized. Raw sewage was no longer accepted. With the incentive of federal funds, two communities joined together in the ecological battle: Kimberly voted to hook up with the Twin Falls sewer system and treatment plant in the Snake River Canyon. The League of Women Voters, who had "just begun to fight" for a new sewage plant in the 1950s, started to win their battle in the 1970s when the city's treatment plant was cited by the EPA (Environmental Protection Agency) for several wastewater discharge violations. The plant was upgraded in 1975 from primary to secondary with a combined waste treatment facility for the city and the industries along Rock Creek Canyon. In 1985 the City Council hired Operations Management International, and OMI brought the sewage plant into compliance with EPA standards and received several awards for its compliance. The cost of the initial improvements and expansion was $8 million; management and operation cost was $2.4 million per year (to 2001).

More Buzz Words: Historic Preservation

Under the Federal Land Policy and Management Act, the Oregon National Historic Trail was established the 1978. In Idaho, which has more intact remnants of the 2,000-mile Oregon Trail than any other state, initial steps were taken to identify and protect its primary route for public use and enjoyment. Very little of the stretch of the Oregon Trail that runs through Twin Falls and the County is evident, however, due to the plow and pavement.

The Twin Falls County Commission became concerned about the destruction and alteration of good historic structures.

> *What bothered me was that the old County Hospital was going to be destroyed—a perfectly good old building.* —Judy Felton (1999)

County Commissioners Judy Felton and Marvin Hempleman knew that for a decade, under the 1966 National Historic Preservation Act, the National Park Service independently—and with the help of Idaho historian Dr. Merle Wells—had designated historic districts and buildings to be considered for the National Register of Historic Places. The idea was to encourage appreciation for, and preservation of, historic structures. So when the original 1918 County Hospital was destroyed in the mid-1980s, the county commission created the Twin Falls County Historic Preservation Commission to save more of the county's historic structures and districts.

Historical Update: The Twin Falls City Park Historic District went on the Register in 1972. Added in 1978 were the 1911 Twin Falls County Courthouse; the 1917 First Presbyterian Church; and the 1908 C. Harvey Smith, Georgian revival-style residence at 255 Fourth Avenue E. Of seven commercial core buildings considered, two were placed on the Register: the 1910 Twin Falls Bank and Trust Building in 1986 and the 1909 Twin Falls Canal Company Building in 1996. In 1990 Lincoln School's 1937 addition was approved, and in 1992 the Lincoln Street electric streetlights, circa 1917, were put on the National Register.

In cases where owners had other plans for considered and/or approved buildings, these structures were not preserved. The Art Deco-style Burkholder Building, one of the seven considered in the commercial core, was razed as were two churches in the City Park Historic District: the Lutheran/Reformed and the LDS First Stake. The 1904 McCollum residence was approved since it was only superficially modified (beyond recognition, now Ann's Eyewear Boutique).

City and County Services Expanded

In 1974 the Twin Falls Fire Department got a new station, designed by local architect Harald Gerber, at 345 Second Avenue E next to the City Hall.

> *Twin Falls is the Idaho city that started the "Learn Not to Burn" program in elementary schools. Bickel Elementary was the pilot school. . . . Our fire runs are way down to this day.*
>
> —Bob K. Bopp, retired fire chief (2001)

At the airport, that fire station's capability was increased by two new trucks: a Quick Response Unit and a foam-spreader that was required by the FHA. SkyWest began flights to Salt Lake City in 1983 through its Delta Connection.

The Twin Falls Police Department moved in 1977 from its old station on Second Street N to its new facility at 356 Third Avenue E, behind the City Hall. The last wall of the old O'Leary Junior High School came down on 3 May 1980, and built on the site in 1989 was the County Courthouse Annex and the new County Jail, which would house the prisoners from the over-crowded top floor of the Courthouse.

The Twin Falls Public Library got a $250,000 building addition in 1974. The next year the historic 1937 section of the Lincoln School got a new addition. Then in 1978 Idaho voters passed the 1.0 percent property tax initiative earmarked for schools, and a new O'Leary Junior High School opened the next year. A new I. B. Perrine Elementary School was built in 1989. Behind then Twin Falls High School a City Pool opened with geothermally heated showers, the only 50-meter, Olympic-sized public pool in Idaho (outside Boise).

The County Hospital "morphed" for a second time in 1982. The 60-bed Magic Valley Memorial Hospital became the 105-bed Magic Valley Regional Medical Center, which in 1997 would be licensed for 173 beds. The acquisition of Canyon View would add 40 beds.

When the Idaho legislature created voluntary health districts in 1947, the cooperative Twin Falls County Public Health unit, begun in 1928, was already functioning in eight counties. This Southcentral District Health was the leader in the multi-county concept. In 1971 the state passed a districting law mandating that the District's structure be adopted throughout Idaho, and every county participated. Southcentral Idaho was the leader which other counties and states across the nation emulated.

Commerce Kept Pace

Right on the heels of the 1970 opening of the downtown Pedestrian Mall was the opening of the Blue Lakes Shopping Center, one block to the north of the Lynwood Shopping Center—no longer on the outskirts of town. The Blue Lakes Shopping Center became an indoor mall in 1978, the first in Southcentral Idaho; two decades later it would be razed and replaced by the Fred Meyers complex.

Some changes and modernization continued downtown after urban renewal. Two 1915 buildings in the 300 block of Main Avenue S were torn down to make way for Emery Petersen's new building and expansion, which included The Boot Shop and The Saddle Shop.

> *Petersen's Western Wear was the largest westernwear store in Southern Idaho, until D & B expanded and moved to the outskirts of town.*
>
> —Emery Petersen (2001)

The Twin Falls Bank and Trust expanded in 1976 into the space formerly occupied by J. J. Newberry and F. W. Woolworth. We saw pioneer Harry Eaton take the job of teller and bookkeeper at the Twin Falls Bank and Trust Company in 1917. Harry worked his way up to chairman of the board and president. Son Curtis T. began working for the company in 1957 and became bank president upon his father's death in 1972.

Lady Bird Johnson's beautification project for interstate highways was eliminating the billboard business. Cosgriff Sign Company, one of the oldest in Idaho, merged in 1975 with the twelve-year-old Moore Sign Company. In 1978 all of Cosgriff's Twin Falls assets, including the building at 260 Second Avenue W, were purchased by Tom Moore.

Bob Latham, son of A. O. "Snowball" and Blanche Latham, became owner of the Bob Reese Motor Company on Main Avenue S for which he had been general manager, and he changed the name to Latham Motors. In the tradition of his generous father, Bob was a Bruins Booster and a major donor to the Special Olympics, the Twin Falls County Fair and Rodeo, and CSI. Bob staged the First Annual Match Play Golf Tournament at the Twin Falls Municipal Golf Course in 1988.

> *I erected that 150-foot flagpole* [at Latham Motors] *with a 40-by-60-foot American flag to show the pride I feel for my country.*
>
> —Bob Latham (2002)

When Tom Koto's brother Ernest died in 1976, Tom sold Koto's Café at 147 Shoshone N (recently A'Roma) to Kay Kawamoto who retained the name. Matsuye (Mrs. Tom) "retired," but Tom stayed on to help out another year, and then he retired after almost fifty years of this pioneer family's business.

Meanwhile, George Kawamoto ran Kay's Supper Club and built George K's on Kimberly Road. Kay sold Koto's Café in 1981 and moved with brother George to Burley to open George K's East. George sold George K's (on Kimberly) to his nephew Kerry Kawamoto in 1986. The brothers would sell George K's East in 1995, and once again residing in Twin Falls, they would retire after forty-three years in the business they built after WWII. Kerry would sell George K's in 1998 at the end of twenty years of a favorite Twin Falls restaurant.

Almost eight decades after townsite businessmen became the Homeless Twenty to improve their new town in the desert, the city's downtown businessmen had a similar club: Twin Falls Futures Unlimited. Its members had familiar names: Cain, Eaton, Allen, Roper, Petersen, Mead, Ashenbrener, and others, who figured they could effect improvements in the downtown. Under the 1980 Idaho Business Improvement District (BID) Law, "the Futures" sought to form a BID which would be supported by dues assessed to the business owners. They held a membership drive, the response was overwhelming, and the City Council created the Twin Falls Downtown BID in 1982.

In 1982 Donna (Mrs. Jack) Scott was elected to the state legislature in Idaho's Twenty-third District. At the end of her term in 1986, Donna became a lobbyist for Tort Reform, "a good thing." Jack Scott sold Scott Polar Corporation (a merger of Scott's Refrigeration and his Polar Manufacturing) to a Canadian company in 1988. The name was retained and so was Jack Scott as president. The next year, Scott joined with Lon Jensen of

Reno to form Scott Jensen Industries to manufacture Ozone Generators for the purification of water. Scott was in business for himself again with a third generation of Scotts coming on line.

Charles and Howard Allen retired in 1988 closing a notable seventy-eight-year history of their one-family Sterling Jewelry business—true Twin Falls pioneer Stickers. In 1989 the First Federal Savings and Loan Association of Twin Falls, which began in 1916 as the Twin Falls Building and Loan Association, became the First Federal Savings Bank of Twin Falls.

Another Drought Hit Farmers; Migrant Workers Got Help

The down side of the forty-to-fifty-year weather cycle hit Idaho farmers in 1977 with the worst drought since the decade of the 1930s with its dust bowl and depression. Economy sagged and credit crunched as the farm recession that followed the drought brought failure and sale of hundreds of farms and out-migration from the area. Grasshoppers invaded in 1985 and more than six million acres of range land were sprayed. The area's longest continuous dry spell of the twentieth century—fifteen years—would not be broken until the record snowfall of the winter of 1992–93.

The Idaho Migrant Council (IMC), which was founded by Humberto Fuentes and opened in Twin Falls in 1971, had three departments: Housing, Headstart, and Employment and Training (E&T). In the 1980s the Twin Falls branch purchased the Migrant Labor Camp, which had fallen into squalor since the 1960s, for emigrant housing. "With a little grant money and a lot of work, we slowly turned it completely around" and renamed it *El Milagro* (the Miracle) that would house three hundred people in 102 units.

> *Emigrants that come to Twin Falls—not just migrant workers and not just Hispanics—come to this E&T Office . . . we are the "clearing house." We provide assistance for all the services needed: Housing, Child Care, Mental Health, as well as E&T. Our goal is to help migrants from the fields, and anyone else who comes to us, find good-paying permanent jobs.*
>
> —Alejandro Castaneda, director of E&T, IMC (2001)

Located at *El Milagro* on Washington Street S was the Felipe Cabral Migrant Headstart named for a Texan emigrant who was a strong advocate of the Headstart program. Sr. Cabral worked in the fields where also he died in 1984.

> *The Hispanic names are misleading in that they may lead one to believe these are programs exclusively for Hispanics. But the names only reflect the initiative and involvement of their Hispanic pioneers.*
>
> —Marisela Lee, Headstart department

Other pioneers were honored during the long drought. For the Twin Falls 75th Anniversary Celebration in 1979, Walter R. Priebe, ninety-nine; Edgar Olmstead, ninety-two; and Otto Florence Sr., ninety-one, shared the honor of Father of the Year. Edgar Olmstead ran a pioneer cattle feeding operation and served on the Twin Falls School Board for many years. Walter Priebe remained an active sportsman until his death in 1987 at age 106. Otto Sr. retired in 1983 when a third generation of Florences bought the Independent Meat Company.

The City of Twin Falls Continued to Lead

Promoting economic development, improving the sewage plant, and boosting the city's water supply and system would be a few of Tom Courtney's successes after taking the position of Twin Falls City Manager in 1980. The typical tenure for this job was eight years; Tom would manage Twin Falls for more than twenty years, advising the city councils and following through with planning objectives. Only two other Idaho cities had city managers, and Tom Courtney would be mentor to both managers.

> *The city's success is because of all the people involved with this city.*
>
> —Tom Courtney (2002)

In 1981 the Twin Falls City Council and Twin Falls County Commission worked out an agreement concerning the "area of impact," which was established under the 1975 State Local Planning and Zoning Act. That act required cities to do long-range planning and to set up an area of impact, one mile wide beyond the city limits, to control growth for the day the area would be incorporated into the city. The city would administer the area's zoning and subdivision regulations and building department codes, and the county's jurisdiction would cover animal regulations and sanitation in agricultural areas over twenty acres. The agreement, which was written into both the city and the county codes, allowed for the Twin Falls County Commission to appoint two members to the City Planning and Zoning Commission (P&Z) from the area of impact and to act upon advice of City Council.

> *Ours is different from other towns' agreements. This city is very lucky in that we have had competent attorneys* [to write the agreement].
>
> —Renee Carraway, P&Z assistant (2001)

The City Council created a new city government agency in 1986, the Economic Development Department (EDD). The first director, Vince Alberdi (now general manager of the Canal Company), was succeeded by Dave McAlindin in September 1988. Also that year Gov. Cecil Andrus (who had just blocked nuclear waste shipments to INEL) signed into law the Local Economic Development Act (LEDA) to provide "tax-increment financing" for cities to use. This turned out to be a key tool in the EDD's strategy to bring in light, non-polluting industry, and Twin Falls was the first city in Idaho to put the LEDA into action.

The EDD could now give the Urban Renewal Agency (URA, 1965) authority to finance economic development. The URA got a new executive director, the same Dave McAlindin, director of EDD, who then "wore both hats." The purpose of the URA became exclusively job creation, mainly through siting and expansion of light manufacturing plants that would also bring additional revenue to the downtown area.

> *The first success was met when Trus-Joint Corporation opened a window-manufacturing plant in South Park.* —*The Times-News*

A working example of LEDA was a project that followed the purchase in 1985 of Consolidated Frozen Foods by Milwaukee-based Universal Foods

Corporation (UFC, now Lamb-Weston, situated above Rock Creek Canyon). In 1989 UFC wanted to make a $22 million expansion to produce four hundred different products and to employ nine hundred people, becoming Twin Falls's largest employer. In exchange for creating this added tax base, URA floated a "tax-increment bond"—and also obtained federal and local grants—to make improvements to the expansion that included a sewage digester, extension of new water and sewer lines, and the Victory Avenue Bridge for a total of $5.5 million.

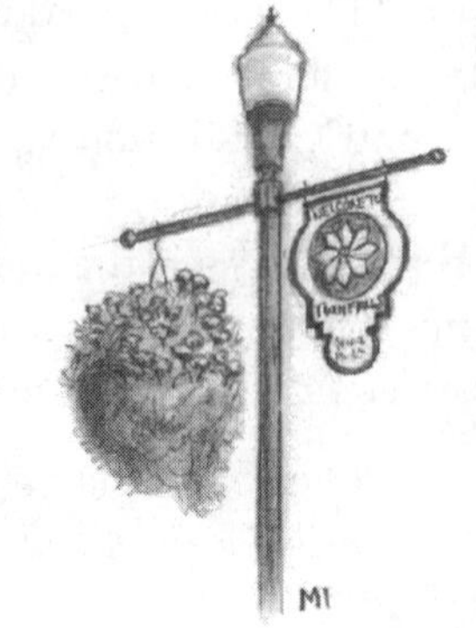

The additional taxes generated by UFC's expansion went toward paying off the tax-increment bond, and any excess went into urban renewal projects such as street lights (e.g., the historical replicas with hanging flower baskets on Shoshone Street), sidewalks, pocket parks, landscaping, and parking lots at no expense to the citizens of Twin Falls. After paying off the twenty-two-year bond, the taxes would revert to the taxing entities that, meanwhile, had been foregoing those property taxes: city, county, highway department, and CSI; taxes were at no time withheld from the public schools.

The College of Southern Idaho Gained Distinction

Under the Federal Older Americans Act of 1965, the Idaho Commission on Aging created the Older Worker Program (OWP) covering Idaho Areas I through VI. CSI became the grantee for the Area IV (Magic Valley) OWP, headquartered at the Idaho Office on Aging on the college campus.

> [Under Peggy Jackson] *our program has ranked first in the nation eight of the last ten years for placement of Older Workers in unsubsidized jobs.* —Dick Boyd, director, Idaho Office on Aging at CSI (2001)

Through another federal law, Twin Falls was chosen to be a community refuge, to give relief and help to refugees in the area from war-torn countries. Ron Black was named director of CSI's Refugee Service Center to provide opportunity and challenge to Twin Falls's newest settlers.

The Herrett Museum, a $6 million facility built with community contributions to display Herrett's Indian collection, was dedicated on 13 June

HERRETT CENTER

1980. CSI acquired Norman Herrett's collection of twenty thousand American Indian artifacts in 1972 and housed it in a small basement facility. Herrett designed and developed the budding museum with young students in mind by using a system of hands-on teaching by teens. The museum also displayed Herrett's original 1960 planetarium instrument. Herrett's wife, Lillie, died in 1974, and Herrett's death followed five years later.

In 1975 archeologist James Woods, a Twin Falls native, was named director of the Herrett Museum. He continued working on projects to learn more about the earliest inhabitants of the Great Basin and of Guatemala. In 1996 James Woods would set up a living exhibit that would earn him the Idaho Humanities Council's top award for Outstanding Achievement in the Humanities.

Historical Update: The world-class Faulkner Planetarium, with computer-graphics-projection capability, was added to the Herrett Center in 1995. After retirement in 1990 from his Paris store, Earl Faulkner became a tireless fund-raiser for the college. Faulkner raised a remarkable amount of money for the College of Southern Idaho Foundation and was largely responsible for the planetarium named for him. One of CSI's three thousand benefactors, Faulkner died in 2001 at age eighty-nine and left his $1.5 million estate to the college in his will. Faulkner's gift, the second largest single gift to the college, would provide for a 24-inch, research-grade telescope with handicap accessibility in 2004.

He said he made his money from the people here, so he meant to leave it here. —Midge Fisher, Paris employee (2001)

The college acquired other adjuncts. Located on the college campus, Frontier Field was added to the City Parks system in a 1974 agreement between the City and the College of Southern Idaho. The Fitness Trail at CSI, financed by the Rotary Club, opened in 1983 for walkers and joggers. Exercise stations were posted along the wood-chip path that wound for 2.1 miles along the Perrine Coulee, through one of the loveliest two-year college campuses to be found anywhere in this country.

In the late 1980s local sheep ranchers John and Miriam Breckenridge donated to CSI hundreds of acres of prime real estate on the north end of town. By exchanging some of that land for cash to put into its education programs, CSI made possible the construction of Target, Costco, and much of the rest of the northside retail complex to develop near the Magic Valley Mall, which opened in 1986. With forty-one stores along their route, anchored by Sears, Bon Marche, and J. C. Penney, four hundred seniors, members of the Mall Walkers Club, made the Magic Valley Mall their circuit in 1989.

Culture and Community Living Were Further Enhanced

New traditions were begun. At CSI, Carson Wong, conductor of the Magic Valley Civic Symphony, instigated in 1974 a biannual Youth Soloist Competition with a prize of $250 to each winner. Finalists would be chosen to perform at the orchestra's October concerts. Wong began the orchestra's Spring Pops Concerts in 1984, and in 1996 he would organize the Magic Valley Youth Orchestra.

The wife of Dr. David A. McClusky, one of the founders of the Twin Falls Clinic and Hospital, started a Christmas tradition while she was serving on the city council from 1977 to 1986. In 1985 Mary McClusky headed the committee to raise money for the town's annual Christmas project: bright, colored lights on eighteen evergreen trees in City Park and live music in the band shell on the four Sundays of Advent. Mary gave Twin Falls a small-town sense of community that would be the envy of any American city. "Our Lady of the Christmas Tree" would pass away in 1999 at the age of eighty.

Marty (Mrs. David) Mead, one of the founders of the Dilettantes, organized the JuMP (Junior Musical Playhouse) Company in 1986 for youngsters to present their own productions—*Snoopy, Huckleberry Finn, Cinderella, Annie*, and others—to an enthusiastic community.

The Magic Valley Arts Council (MVAC) was reorganized in 1988. A better balance of managers and visionaries was created for support of the Arts and improvement of community living. To feature local artists MVAC opened Twin Falls's first and only art museum. The Arts Council presented both the first Arts on Tour program and the first Foreign Film Festival in 1987. In 1989 MVAC started the annual Kids Art in the Park and in 1993 would co-sponsor the three-year-old Hispanic Heritage Fiesta.

Chapter 16

Decade of the '90s

Unemployment in the Magic Valley reached a thirty-year low of 4.1 percent; non-farm employment grew by 3.5 percent—not the estimated 2.7 percent; and . . . the farm economy continued to sag.

Twin Falls's Economy Boomed with the Country's

Two new manufacturers were established in Twin Falls with the help of the EDD's "tax-for-improvements" program administered by the URA: Seastrom Manufacturing, maker of precision parts from California, and Clear Shield (now Solo Cup), a plastic cutlery factory. Lamb-Weston, a maker of french fries owned by Con-Agra, purchased Universal Foods in 1994 and continued to be Twin Falls's largest employer. In 1997 Irish-owned Avonmore Foods, largest cheese-maker in the Northwest and third largest in the United States, bought the Twin Falls Cheese plant, then changed its name to Glanbia Foods. The Eastern Idaho Railroad Company bought most of Union Pacific's Magic Valley lines. And also, the 750 farmers from Nampa to Blackfoot who had formed a growers' co-op three years earlier purchased Amalgamated Sugar Company in 1997.

The Hispanic population was the fastest growing in the Magic Valley and accounted for 16 percent of small business starts. The senior population sector also grew, and CSI tapped into it. Enrollment of senior students sixty-five years and older increased from 1.7 percent in 1990 to 4.5 percent in 1998.

The Twin Falls Public Library got a new addition in 1990; the architect and the local architectural consultant were Richardson and Associates of Salt Lake City and Harald Gerber, AIA, of Twin Falls. In 1994 Twin Falls

High School got the new 1,335-seat (John) Roper Auditorium, named to honor one of Twin Falls's outstanding citizens.

Harald Gerber also designed Joslin Field's new 1996 terminal, and local artist Gary Stone painted the terminal's ceiling with a great variety of aircraft and a wall with a historical mural. For ten years, Horizon Airlines had supplied Twin Falls with flights to Boise on small 19-seat Fairchild Metros. In 1997 Horizon dropped the small planes, moved to the larger DeHavilland–8, and left the Twin Falls market. Meanwhile, SkyWest continued its flights to Salt Lake City through its Delta Connection.

We are trying to bring back service to Boise with the smaller planes.

—Bill Carberry, manager, Twin Falls Regional Airport (2003)

Also in 1997, long-distance tolls were dropped as toll-free calling was extended to fourteen Magic Valley communities due to the campaign waged by Jean Duffek(-Nutsch), a Jerome resident and Twin Falls native. The Twin Falls Fire Department bought a new E-1 (Emergency One) Custom Pumper costing $276,451.50, and Lamb-Weston donated its HAZMAT (hazardous materials) trailer to the Fire Department in October 1999.

Ecology and Heritage Merged

Tourism is now the world's number one industry.

—Stephen Richards, president of Elderhostel, Inc. (1998)

Eco-tourism was still the largest stimulus for recreational travel in the United States in the 1990s, but the Idaho Travel Council reported that heritage-tourism was a close second. This drew attention again to the Oregon Trail which runs through Twin Falls. The Oregon Trail Sesquicentennial in 1993, celebrating the Great Migration of 1843, was observed nationally with a wagon train. Starting at Independence, Missouri, and ending at Oregon City, Oregon, the wagon train came through Twin Falls in July, drawing crowds along the way.

Two sites on the Snake River—Twin Falls's "natural/heritage resource"—got protection after the Idaho State Centennial in 1990 drew attention to the river's significance, both its historic role in the establishment of the state and its singular role in nature. A push began in the 1980s to acquire Box Canyon for a state park.

Located in the Thousand Springs corridor—home to eleven of North America's twenty largest springs—Box Canyon historically yields the largest springs from a single source in the United States churning out 180,000 gallons per minute. —Julie Fanselow, author (1995)

The commercial trout business had matured into a world-class aquiculture industry during the 1970s after hatchery developers bought up and developed most of the available springs along the Snake River, including Box Canyon. After passage of legislation, public involvement with a lawsuit, and a court injunction in 1989, Box Canyon State Park was created in 1999 with the help of The Nature Conservancy.

The second Snake River site that got protection was one-half mile downstream from the Perrine Bridge. The Auger Falls, site of proposed private power plants over many decades, were once again threatened in the 1990s by the Salt Lake City-based Cogeneration Company. A bitter battle was fought by the public in the hearings held in Twin Falls. The Federal Energy Regulatory Commission (FERC) canceled Cogeneration's license in 2000, and there would be no power plant at scenic Auger Falls where the river would continue to run free.

Auger Falls will be protected for generations to come.

—Sara Denniston, Idaho Rivers United

Scenic Snake River got protection from two more parks. The 25-acre Twin Falls County Centennial Waterfront Park below the Perrine Bridge was completed in 1992 as a project of the Rotary Club, and a group of 230 LDS (Latter Day Saints, or Mormon) kids cleaned up a stretch of the canyon east of the park and bridge to established a trail. The last city park acquisition in this decade was made by easement and land trade for the west section of the Snake River Canyon Rim Trail. This parkway started at the north end of Washington Street and proceeded eastward one-half mile along the rim of the canyon to just beyond the Perrine Coulee, giving the public spectacular views. Plans were made to extend the trail to Shoshone Falls. Jerome County would make similar plans for preserving the north rim from Auger Falls to Hansen Bridge.

Historical Update: Of historical interest is the fact that one hundred years after "Congress's threat to create a national park preserve along the Middle Snake River," which Congress then dropped in favor of irrigation, the people of the Magic Valley themselves are bringing that park preserve concept into reality and are actually enlarging upon it—a tribute to their heritage and a legacy for future generations.

Rock Creek Got Attention in Support of Ecology

Twin Falls owned a 1.6-mile stretch of Rock Creek Canyon from the Singing Bridge (which was replaced by the Old Towne Bridge in 1995) almost to Addison Avenue W. During the Great Depression, a shantytown took root there; and the canyon was still being used as a dump into the 1990s. Robin (Mrs. Bob) Seastrom had been involved in civic projects where she came from in California, and she wanted to get involved in Twin Falls. Seastrom took her offer to Mayor Howard Allen who put her in charge of cleaning up the city's stretch of Rock Creek. Robin asked for volunteers, and Beth Sigler, Don Zuck, Les Hazen, David Mead, Steve Soran, Jack Wright, John Pohlman, Howard Allen, and others, pulled hundreds of discarded tires out of Rock Creek that spring of 1993.

It was incredible how much junk we found down there.

—LaMar Orton, director, Twin Falls Planning and Zoning

With the clean-up off to a good start, the City Council created the Old Towne Coalition to convert Rock Creek Canyon, which bordered on Old Towne, into a parkway trail. This coalition was then incorporated as the non-profit Old Towne Corporation, which hired the consultant team of Moscow-based Tom Hudson and Seattle-based Ron Jelaco to plan the historic Old Towne area. Also out of this corporation's agenda came the Rock Creek Brigade in 1995, a coalition of twenty-one entities—hospital, college, banks, sugar factory, Lamb-Weston, etcetera—each subscribing to one-tenth mile of the canyon to keep clean.

Meanwhile, the Parks and Recreation Department ran the "bad element" out of the canyon and made it safe for the public. In response to numerous complaints of sewer odors, the city replaced the old sewer line along a part of that stretch of Rock Creek. The Old Towne Corporation provided financing for benches, trees, paving, and for restoring the canyon's ecology by the removal of exotic species and replacing them with native trees. The result was the Rock Creek Canyon Parkway, alternately called "Old Towne Parkway," a wonderful nature walk along a cool canyon creek on the edge of town, complete with whistling rock chucks and singing birds. (And if you see a beaver, please report it. Although native, beavers are a tree-damaging nuisance and are being controlled in the area.)

Seastrom's original volunteers continued to hold clean-up parties several times a year to haul away tires, shopping carts, mattresses, appliances large and small, and other litter. Beginning in 2001, groups of junior high school students would join the volunteers to spread gravel on side trails and help with general clean-up as part of their annual Helping Hands Week.

> *We thought we needed to keep the spirit alive and to get more volunteers involved.* —John Pohlman, supervisor, Lamb-Weston's Waste Water

Cleaning up part of middle Rock Creek did not solve the pollution problem that had always plagued Rock Creek, nor did it open Rock Creek for swimming. A task force was appointed by the County Commission to make a tour of inspection of the lands along upper Rock Creek for signs and sources of contamination.

> *It's pretty evident that cattle are the main source. The problem is the management of little ranchettes—two to five acres on the canyon wall with small herds of animals.*
>
> —Marvin Hempleman, Twin Falls County commissioner (2002)

Full Attention Went to Recreation

Idaho's Recreation and Tourism Act of 1983 divided the state into six regions, and Southcentral Idaho's Middle Snake River was designated as Region IV. With funding, support, and guidance from the Rivers, Trails, and Conservation Assistance Program of the National Park Service, a Region

IV Recreation Forum was created in the 1990s. Notices were sent to the public, and tours were conducted by courtesy of state grants obtained by the Twin Falls Area Chamber of Commerce. Hearings were held in towns from American Falls to Bliss for public input concerning recreation usage of the river. Citizen volunteers and representatives of all local, state, and federal agencies met to work on the project, facilitated by Mike Pepper of Jerome.

Some Twin Falls citizens were concerned about the steady loss of access to the Snake River for recreational purposes. Don Zuck, retired director of County Parks, formed the Access Committee, and Zuck, Les Hazen, and Bob Lunty did an on-site access inventory of the entire Middle Snake River; Idaho Power did the database work on all sites and locations; and BLM did the mapping and printing.

In 1998 the Forum published its compiled information into a booklet with a map of the Middle Snake River showing ownership of the lands and recreation areas, trails and accesses, existing and proposed. The purpose of the publication was to guide planning and zoning departments in Region IV in their consideration of applications for buildings and other developments along the river. Region IV, the Middle Snake River with Twin Falls as its base, was the only region out of the six to do such a recreation project under Idaho's Recreation and Tourism Act of 1983.

Also in this decade the Twin Falls Parks and Recreation Department got additions and attention. Clyde Thomsen Park was created in 1996 on thirteen acres donated by four Twin Falls citizens. After Arbor Day was celebrated on 27 April 1999, Dennis Bowyer, superintendent of Parks and Rec, received the Tree City USA award for Twin Falls from the National Arbor Day Foundation. Certain requirements had been met by the City Council including passing a tree ordinance and creating a Tree Commission under the Parks and Recreation Department. With David Mead as chairman, the Tree Commission developed a manual, *Tree Selection Guide*, to educate the public and the government about proper selection, care, and maintenance of trees and shrubs and about the problems trees can create. Tree City USA was sponsored by the Idaho Department of Lands and U S Bank. The first Arbor Day was in 1872.

City Pool got a cover in 1999 due to the efforts of a citizens' Cover the Pool Committee led by Stephanie Crumrine that started in 1995 to raise the necessary funds. The cover extended use of the Olympic-sized pool to year around.

Business, But Not as Usual

The small city of Twin Falls—1990 census, twenty-eight thousand—took on all the trappings of a big city. North of Addison Avenue along Blue Lakes Boulevard where stately residences once graced the town's north boulevard approach, a 2-mile strip was already blossoming with national fast-food, eatery, and motel chains, and automobile dealerships. The eighty-year-old shade trees that lined the boulevard were sacrificed to gain a fifth lane, a center turn lane. The vast Magic Valley Mall at the north end of Blue Lakes Boulevard saw "big box" national chain stores come in. In an attempt at reasonable control of this rapid commercial development, City Council passed ordinances that established setbacks, mandated landscaping, and prohibited flashing and rotating signs; an exemption was applied later to the time, temperature, and message center signs.

> *Let's not kid ourselves, it's more difficult now for the little guy to compete. One way for a small business to survive is to provide excellent service . . . to establish a niche.* —Emery Petersen (1998)

Downtown suffered a major upset, and recovered.

> *The downtown is the heart of the city. When a city loses its downtown, it loses its heart.* —City Planning Research

For two decades urban renewal had staved off the loss of downtown businesses, but in the 1990s a toll was taken by several factors: commercial development along Blue Lakes Boulevard and at the north end of town ("big city magnets"); competition from discounters, catalogs, and the Internet; and . . . the depressed farm economy. In 1998 Emery Petersen retired ending fifty-two years of the Petersen family's marketing of superb westernwear. The next year Roper's Clothing Store, anchor downtown retailer started by John Roper, went out of business after fifty years of serving several generations of Twin Falls customers with a high-class line of merchandise.

> *It was an extremely painful decision that was delayed for many years and made after an unsuccessful effort to sell the stores* [in Twin Falls, Burley, and Boise]. —Jim Roper and sons David and Jeff Roper

> *They* [the Ropers] *are part of what made Twin Falls what it is . . . the kind of people who care about the town.*
>
> —Dave Nelson, Sav-Mor Drugs

The huge hole that was created so suddenly in the commerce on Main Avenue would be filled by more specialty shops. Herrett's Jewelry moved into the Paris Building in 1996, and after twenty-six years with Herrett's, Randy's Jewelry would move to 127 Main E in 2002. Tri-Valley Custom Furniture would locate at 161 Main E. The vacated Roper Building would welcome Cathy Reitz's Stitchin' Time and Scott Baument's Christian Book Store in 2001.

> *The big guys don't sell everything the people want. What we're looking for in downtown are stores with good quality specialty items.*
>
> —Tom Ashenbrener, Price Hardware (1998)

After the addition of several new banks, the downtown would be confirmed as Twin Falls's banking center.

More than Ever, Traditions Were Preserved

> *There's a lot about Twin Falls that shouldn't change—such as civility and small-town atmosphere.* —Brent White, manager, Magic Valley Mall

On baseball game days before World War I, Twin Falls businesses closed so everybody could go to the baseball games. In the 1980s the Twin Falls County Fair held "Twin Falls Days," and businesses and the county courthouse closed on those days to allow employees to take in the festivities. But those Days were discontinued in the 1990s and the state government no longer allowed the county courthouse to close completely for anything. So, the courthouse began closing for half a day and rotating its services to allow employees to enjoy the Twin Falls County Fairs; some downtown businesses followed suit, and a small town tradition was preserved.

Twin Falls families continued their long tradition of community service. One such family, the Eatons, grew with the Twin Falls Bank and Trust Company after Harry Eaton joined it in 1917. In 1990 that company merged with the First Security Corporation. Son Curtis T. Eaton became chairman of the board and CEO of First Security; his son Curtis H. was named vice chairman and president. After another merger in 2001, the First Security Bank would become the Wells Fargo Bank. Curtis H. Eaton would leave the family banking business of eighty-four years to become CSI's vice president of Institutional Planning and Development and executive director of the College of Southern Idaho Foundation. Eaton, whose mother was a noted educator, would resign his senior position on the Idaho State Board of Education after a long and distinguished service under three governors.

Otto Florence Jr., retired owner of the Independent Meat Company, received the Lifetime Achievement Award from the Twin Falls Chamber of Commerce in 1992. This family firm would continue to make outstanding contributions to the community by supporting the FFA (Future Farmers of America) and 4H programs and co-sponsoring with CSI the livestock judging competitions among collegiate teams throughout Western United States. Howard Allen, who retired his family's Sterling Jewelry store in 1988, received the Lifetime Achievement Award in 1996. Howard was elected to the city council in 1991, was mayor 1991–92 and, as of this writing, still serves on the council.

CSI student Gloria Galan founded the Hispanic Heritage Fiesta in 1990 and was its president. Working from scratch, Galan's entire family—nine brothers and sisters, nephews and nieces—put together a parade and a fair with traditional Hispanic musicians and dancers, food booths, children's games, a flea market, a low-rider auto show, and a Mexican rodeo at the Twin Falls fairgrounds.

> *We want to keep our culture. The population in this area is not so much Mexicans anymore but a lot of Hispanics that were born and raised here.*
> —Gloria Galan (2002)

The initial Hispanic fiesta that was held in 1957 grew into *Cinco de Mayo*, which is an annual Mexican celebration; Gloria's new Fiesta was held in August to preserve a distinctly Hispanic tradition. Gloria would continue as its president for twelve years to be succeeded in 2002 by Jose Perez, owner of Garibaldi's Mexican Restaurant.

In the Great Depression years, Twin Falls had big-hearted "Joe" Koehler and "Snowball" Latham. Since then, their tradition of generosity and community service was represented by Paul Reynolds and by Randy Hansen, among many others. Reynolds owned the Reynolds Funeral Chapel, which his father James Reynolds started downtown in 1938 and moved to East Addison Road in 1958. Whenever Paul heard that someone was down on his luck, he would fill up the poor guy's gas tank and take him out to breakfast. Paul helped to start St. Edward's Dining Room for the Needy in 1988 and would keep the pantry shelves stocked out of his own pocket. Until his death in 2003 at age sixty, Paul would be a youth activity booster and Valley House supporter.

> *I always felt I had an obligation to give back to the community that has given me so much.* —Paul Reynolds

Randy Hansen's interest in civic service started with the Library Expansion Committee, and he rescued a dying Western Days with a large donation. After purchasing his father's Chevrolet dealership in 1985, Hansen gave away sixteen cars—one raffled off each year—to high school seniors who stayed all night at their graduation parties at CSI.

> *There have been no wrecks or arrests* [on party night] *since.*
> —Randy Hansen

Hansen's list went on: Boy Scouts master, Valley House instigator and president, state legislator for the 1999–2000 term from which he resigned to become a bishop in the Mormon Church. Hansen loved serving and was impressed with the "strength and stability of Magic Valley." In 2002 Randy would be the corporate sponsor and activities chairman for the Olympic Torch Run through Twin Falls.

Hansen's Valley House was a community effort. In 1993 Randy Hansen organized the many groups that traditionally helped the homeless—separately, but inadequately. A group of people from this new organization purchased an old motel at 507 Addison Avenue W and did the reconstruction work. In 1995 Valley House opened to shelter the homeless for short-term until they could get back on their feet. Between 1995 and 2001, more than 1573 people would be housed in the large house and eleven cottages. Valley House would get no tax dollars

and be entirely supported by the community; the same people that started the project would serve on its board.

> *I had the vision we could do it, but all these people with kind hearts deserve the accolades.* —Randy Hansen, president, 1994–97

> *The Valley House philosophy is "A hand up, not a hand-out."*
> —Jeff Gooding, president after 2000

The Twin Falls tradition of outreach and generosity expanded. Habitat for Humanity of Magic Valley (HFH-MV) was incorporated on 26 December 1990 by Tim Dodd, Rev. Ed Pangburn, and Arlan Call, with attorney Britt Groom its first secretary. HFH-MV is governed by a local volunteer board but is an affiliate of Habitat for Humanity International founded in 1976 as a nonprofit ecumenical Christian housing ministry dedicated to eliminating substandard housing and homelessness worldwide.

> *Since 1991, HFH-MV has built three homes on land donated by the city of Twin Falls and is currently constructing two homes under the direction of builder Chuck Taylor who is working closely with the selected families and other volunteers.*
> —Carol Robertson, board member (2002)

Future-Planning Included Tradition and Preservation

The Old Towne Corporation started the future-planning of Twin Falls in 1994 by hiring consultants Hudson and Jelaco. Under their plan, infra-structure improvements were made to the city's Blue Lakes water supply with new wells, some of which raised the water pressure in the southeast part of town to facilitate development in that sector. The wells at Washington Street S and at Hankins Road brought the city's total to ten wells out of the Snake River Plain Aquifer. In 1998 the City Council hired the Colorado-based firm of Balloffet and Associates to draw up a Second-Century Plan. In addition to improvement of the infrastructure they aimed at preserving local quality of life as it pertained to business, recreation, and historical preservation. A long series of public hearings were held to get Twin Falls residents' visions of the city's ideal future. In support of future-planning, Old Towne property owners created an Old Towne BID.

A second historic preservation commission was created. Ron Stanley, owner of the 1906 Twin Falls Milling and Elevator Company's 1912 warehouse, had his building put on the National Register of Historic Places in 1995. The next year, the Twin Falls Historic Warehouse District was placed on the National Register through the efforts of the Twin Falls County Historic Preservation Commission (TFCHPC). The City Council decided that the Warehouse District should be recognized as a *city* rather than a *county* entity, and the Council created the Twin Falls City Historic Preservation Commission in 1997.

I think people will go to places of historic importance.

—Paul Smith, chairman of TFCHPC
and owner of the Historic Canal Company Building

The new city commission was very concerned about the historic preservation of downtown. They arranged to get city funds, a grant from the National Park Service, and approval from the Idaho State Historical Society (ISHS) to hire a preservation planner to study the feasibility of creating a historic downtown district. Elizabeth Giraud from Salt Lake City did a detailed historical examination of fifty-eight downtown properties of which forty-four were found eligible for nomination to the National Register of Historic Places: built at least fifty years before, with minimum subsequent changes made. Giraud completed her study in 1999 and approval was obtained from ISHS and NPS. The designation of Twin Falls Historic Downtown District was established by city ordinance on 13 March 2000. In 2001 the Downtown BID and Old Towne BID would merge to combine both historic districts under one name: Twin Falls Historic Old Towne.

ON THE NATIONAL REGISTER

Downtown is still unique. People like that environment.

—Randy Bombardier, BID

History and tradition were preserved through restoration. After selling his Crowley's pharmacy in 1998, third generation Richard Crowley restored his remaining business in the Booth Building, which was remodeled during urban renewal. In the spirit of revitalization and preservation, Crowley removed carpet and linoleum to reveal the original wooden floor and restored the ceiling to the original sculptured tin. He moved the "old fashioned" soda fountain, which had languished in the rear of the store, to the front and gave it top billing of what became Crowley's Soda Fountain and General Store. His pride and joy was on the exposed brick firewall behind the fountain: Norman Rockwell's painting *The Soda Jerk*, to which Crowley owned sole marketing rights. A traditional meeting place, Crowley's remained a Twin Falls landmark.

> *I wanted to capitalize on this old tradition . . . to keep the history alive in downtown. . . . We could have sold the building, but we are downtowners at heart. It's part of our heritage.*
>
> —Richard Crowley (1998)

Andy Crane purchased the 1920 Elks Lodge and restored the former dance hall to accommodate 380 people. Discotech dances were held on Wednesday nights, and other cultural events were planned to make the Elks once again a community hall. Crane planned to restore the front to its original façade and applied for a listing on the National Register.

> *History is good for business.* —*The Times-News*

Hoops's Rogerson Mall (formerly Rogerson Hotel) and Motel Inn, which had been sitting virtually vacant on the market for five years, were purchased in 1999 by Glenn and Judy Schroeder after a title complication was resolved. They planned to remodel the mall for new tenants and tear down the old motel in back, but they needed financing. Urban Renewal Agency went to the rescue. The Schroeders tore down the motel behind the mall and URA purchased the property for a parking lot and pocket park for the amount of the Schroeder's cost, up to $255,000.

I think part of the success is the Urban Renewal Agency's willingness to participate with the investors . . . if they're willing to invest.

—Dave McAlindin, director, URA (2000)

A Decade, A Century, and A Millennium Ended in Apprehension

Craig Neilsen submitted plans in 1999 for a 10-story hotel, a 15,000-square-foot convention center, and a large retail complex on his Snake River Canyon rim property west of the Buzz Langdon Visitor Center. Neilsen asked the City Council for changes in the Canyon Rim Overlay Zone Ordinance, which had established a set-back of one hundred feet and a height limit of thirty-five feet, to accommodate his plans. When the public hearings were packed with angry protesters, the City Council formed a citizens design committee to review rim building plans and to advise the Planning and Zoning Commission. The next year, Mayor Gale Kleinkopf established the Canyon Hotel Design Review Commission with members Tom Mikesell, Kevin Dane, David Mead, Stephanie Crumrine, and Brent Jussel. Their mission statement included such guidelines:

shall not impair or preclude the orderly and harmonious development of the community . . . the topography of the Snake River Canyon is not rectangular in nature . . . the canyon has no vertical lines that reach from top to bottom . . . the canyon has many elevations, plateaus, recesses, at differing heights . . . it has shadows and relief . . . it has neutral as well as warm natural colors.

Concern over community values and political direction prompted candidates and provoked voters in Twin Falls. In the November 1999 city council election, a woman, Glenda Thompson, challenged a long-term incumbent and another candidate for one seat, and won. Hispanic candidate Gloria Galan was challenged by a man for a vacant seat, and she won. This put three women on the 7-man council, a new milestone for Twin Falls. It also looked like the one incumbent councilwoman, the former BID director Elaine Steele, just might become Twin Falls's first woman mayor.

Chapter 17

A New Millennium, a New Century

The middle class is shrinking. —2000 Census

The middle is disappearing.

—Pat Takasugi, director, Idaho Department of Agriculture

"Y2K" Stood for the Year 2000

The twenty-first century brought soaring natural gas prices that were followed by sky-rocketing wholesale electricity prices due to deregulation of the industry. Blackouts rolled through California. Still, Idaho maintained the lowest energy costs of all the fifty states in spite of having the second highest gasoline prices. Then, by July 2001, energy prices dropped due to conservation efforts, re-regulation, and the actions of energy producers.

In Twin Falls County the disparity between rich and poor increased by 1.68 percent. Lower wages, second jobs, and multiple-income families were still realities of life in Magic Valley. Median income was 82 percent of the U.S. median, but cost of living was 94 percent of the national average. In the 1990s Twin Falls County grew 20 percent, Twin Falls city about 25 percent dropping to seventh largest city in the state while Idaho grew 28.5 percent, the fifth fastest growing state.

The Hispanic population, the fastest growing ethnic group in the United States, grew by 50 percent in Idaho between 1990 and 1996 and was still growing by 8 percent in 2000, which made Twin Falls County No. 5.

A lot of growth is coming from within, [not from immigration].

—Gladys Esquibel, chairman, Idaho Commission on Hispanic Affairs (2000)

Roughly 35 to 40 percent of Idaho's Hispanic population worked on farms. Thirty of the farm operators in Twin Falls County were Hispanic or of Latin origin in 2000.

That year brought drought so severe that the Twin Falls Canal Company reduced water delivery and Idaho Power Company paid irrigators to reduce their electricity consumption. The grim water situation, which peaked in August 2000, was exacerbated by heat; August 2001 was the second hottest in thirty years—El Niño was blamed. Summer 2002 was the third hottest on record after 1936 and 1934, dust bowl years. The average stream flow at Milner Dam did not exceed 2,000 cubic feet per second again until the rainy spring of 2003, and Shoshone Falls then went from dry to a trickle.

Grain prices that had collapsed in 1998 were at a thirty year low. Lands once in spud farms that had gone on the auction block were left fallow or put into feed grains, hay, and silage to supply the growing dairy industry. By 2002, many small farms had been replaced by large Concentrated Animal Feeding Operations (CAFOs), some having as many as nine thousand cows.

The Drought of 2000 Brought Wildfires

Devastating wildfires in 2000 were the worst since 1910, and even worse in 2002 with extreme drought and heat. Local businessmen once again served the firefighters. In August 2000 Steve Soran, who served fire sites since 1962, catered twenty-four fires and fed crews from Arkansas, Alaska, Colorado, Oregon, and Washington. Jim Vickers supplied boots to the Malta fire site; only a few dealers carried these specialty boots designed for firefighting. Neither Soran nor Vickers charged extra or mark-up at these times of disaster. Les Reitz of PSI sent portable toilets and garbage cans to twelve sites. Their services were repeated in 2002.

THE SORANS
FIGHT WILDFIRE

> *It* [wildfire] *is good business, but I don't know how many people would do what we do.* —Jim Vickers, Vickers Western Store

To aid in wildfire fighting, the city built a tanker-loading facility at Joslin Field on a lease agreement with the BLM (Bureau of Land Management), which kept storage tanks of water and fire retardant there. During the fire season, the BLM had a firefighting helicopter stationed at Jerome, and at Joslin Field had a jump plane and two contracted single-engine air tankers (SEATS). In addition was an air-attack platform for aerial supervision.

> *This platform is a fixed-wing plane that flies above the fire to assist in coordinating relief efforts between the ground crews and the other aircraft.* —Larry Mabbutt, unit aviation manager, BLM (2003)

Twin Falls Economy Continued To Be Strong

March 2001 started the recession that ended ten years of expansion with the "New Economy" based on information and services. In the following months, the Federal Reserve cut prime interest rates a record eleven times to reach 1.75 percent, the lowest in forty years. Due to the largest corporation bankruptcy in history in 2002 with Enron's accounting scandals and others, loss of faith in Wall Street—and low interest rates—turned investors to real estate and housing. Of Idaho cities surveyed that year about home mortgage payments, Twin Falls had the lowest principle and interest: near 6.5 percent, which went on to a record low of 5.31 percent in May 2003. The Twin Falls construction sector grew in strength to top the state.

> *State leaders called the Twin Falls area one of Idaho's economic engines.* —*The Times-News*

The shocking terrorist acts on 11 September 2001, called "9-11," brought down the Twin Towers of the World Trade Center in New York City, damaged the Pentagon in Washington D.C., and cratered the ground in Pennsylvania with a loss of 3,025 innocent lives. Suddenly, the New Economy was replaced by a "Security Economy" based on security and confidence with a wide range of costly upgrades such as airport and building security. Yet, through all the negatives of a national downturn, the Twin Falls economy appeared to be insulated.

Twin Falls Responded to the Threat of Terrorism.

> *When Company D 321st Engineers first met, it was in a crummy building on East Kimberly Road. Then in the 1980s, Bob Gillespie and I started the process of establishing the reserve center that was built at Joslin Field.* —Col. Joe Eyre, retired, Army Reserve Ambassador for the State of Idaho (2003)

Then for years, Company D 321st Engineers was housed at the Allred U.S. Army Reserve Center at Joslin Field. But in 2000, with only five reservists training there, the center closed and the local reservists made long drives on weekends to Boise and Pocatello for training. With the terrorist acts of 9-11, interest in all branches of service went up 50 percent, and four months later the center was reactivated. In January 2002 about thirty local reservists plus the 1016th Quartermaster Detachment from Pocatello again trained at Joslin Field.

The Twin Falls airport was one of the first twenty-three airports nationwide chosen by the federal government to be restructured for security. Under the Homeland Securities Act of 2002, Twin Falls airport was one of 429 commercial airports to take on federal security responsibilities. Transportation Security Administration screeners provided friendly customer service and strict security measures; Joslin Field got a remodeling job to create office and break areas for about twelve screeners.

More locals were getting on Greyhound, which moved its station from 461 Second Avenue S (after thirty years) to North Blue Lakes. Since 9-11, the bus front seats were off limits to passengers.

One year after the anthrax scare that followed 9-11, Southcentral District Health formed an Office of Public Health Response to respond to outbreaks of disease or acts of bio-terrorism. With a Center for Disease Control (CDC) grant, it would coordinate programs . . .

> *to continue the ongoing epidemiological surveillance and disease investigation roles of the District.* —Monie Smith, public information officer, Southcentral District Health (2003)

Twin Falls Saw Mergers and Global Trade. One economic trend at the turn of the century was mergers of gigantic size. Twin Falls saw two mergers: First Security Bank became Wells Fargo Bank, and U S West (local and in fourteen states) became Qwest Communications International, both were Denver based.

Another trend was the growth of global markets, which outpaced domestic markets. Twin Falls's Independent Meats and Hamilton Manufacturing went global. Ben Homma of Shentoa International of Japan said he "can drum up all the demand Independent Meats can supply." Hamilton, with its cellulose insulation and hydro-seeding mulch made from recycled paper, was contacted by Japanese, Shanghi, and Philippine companies. Business was brisk, as Hamilton's inventory was being depleted for rehab seeding after the devastating wildfires of 2000 and 2001. Hamilton's CEO Tamara Hamilton-Harvey and her husband moved to Michigan, but the company stayed.

> *The international business stays in Twin Falls because it can't get Twin Falls-style hometown support anywhere else.*
>
> —Tamara Hamilton-Harvey (2001)

The Arts Contributed to the Local Economy. As a tool to attract companies, the Arts made a contribution to the strength of the local economy. The Magic Valley Arts Council hired Ted Clausen of Boston in May 2000 to design a centennial sculpture. The 2-part bronze and rock sculpture, one section at the city center and the other in City Park, was dedicated on 10 May 2001.

> *Culture-tourism is big money.*
>
> —Dan Harpole, Idaho Commission on the Arts

New Organizations and a New Industry

The Twin Falls Area Chamber of Commerce followed its Business Plus I with Business Plus II, a $1.5 million economy-and-community-development campaign. In conjunction with CSI, Business Plus II created the South Idaho Economic Development Organization (SIEDO) to recruit small manufacturers to bring new jobs to Magic Valley, and to retain those established by using incentive grants. This 2-county effort (Twin Falls and Jerome) was a coalition of public and private sector leaders with Jan Rogers its executive director. One thousand new jobs were created.

Twin Falls was one of 3,300 communities (!) that Dell Computer Corporation of Texas considered in 2000 for a call center. The City Council, with URA and SIEDO, assembled a "creative and responsive" incentive package for Dell that they could not refuse, and in 2001 Twin Falls was chosen. A lot of cities made a lot of promises but:

> *Twin Falls is the only one that delivered. . . . They were very impressed with the high school level of computer competency.*
>
> —Greg Rogers, Idaho Department of Labor

> *Getting Dell was getting back to the original purpose* [under EDD] *of the Urban Renewal Agency: job creation. Dell* [who promised 700 jobs] *had to have the Albertson Building* [at the north end of Blue Lakes Boulevard, not downtown].
>
> —Dave McAlindin, director, URA and EDD

By the end of 2002, Dell had created 727 full-time jobs with good pay and benefits. In 2003 Business Plus III expanded to include six of the Magic Valley counties (excluded were Blaine, Camas, and Elmore). The target of this five-year, $1.44 million campaign was two thousand jobs with an annual salary of $22,500.

Like Tom Courtney, who in his first twenty years as city manager became mentor to the managers of two other Idaho cities, Dave McAlindin, director of the Urban Renewal Agency since 1989, became a mentor in 2003. The Blackfoot URA, viewing their Twin Falls counterpart as a model, consulted with McAlindin concerning his agency's history and projects.

> *I'm thrilled they think enough of us to come and ask questions.*
>
> —Dave McAlindin

ARTEC Had the Solution.

> *What the valley has is plenty of dependable, eager, and honest workers. What the valley needs is more worker training.*
>
> —Greg Rogers, Idaho Job Service

In 1998, area businesses and twenty school districts formed a regional technical high school consortium known as ARTEC: Advanced Regional Technical Education Coalition. Funding was from Albertson Foundation grants, school districts, and Business Plus II. The Twin Falls School District's trial run enrolled two dozen students in classes held at CSI. The second year, classes were held in the high school, and by fall 2000, 840 students were enrolled. Students in ARTEC programs learned academics while being equipped for the high skilled and changing demands of the labor force that they would enter right out of high school.

Commerce Expanded into New Locations. In May 2002 the Weston Plaza Hotel and Convention Center (formerly the Holiday Inn, one of the first to appear on North Blue Lakes in the 1970s), was torn down. Neilsen's 40-acre Canyon Park Shopping Center on the Snake River Canyon rim east of the Perrine Bridge opened with national chain stores and restaurants. With the North Blue Lakes Boulevard strip full, commercial growth of small businesses went eastward on Addison Avenue—the second most traveled street in Twin Falls—to Eastland Drive. A retail strip grew east of Eastland across from K-Mart where Koppel's Browzeville moved from downtown and changed its name to Backcountry Outfitters. Jim Vickers opened his new store there stating that "Vickers Western Store had outgrown its 1920s building in Old Towne, and it was starting to need repair."

Based on Twin Falls economic growth, Iowa-based Lee Enterprises purchased *The Times-News*, No. 16 of Howard Publications, in November 2002. Although jobless rates were super-low, overall job growth ground to a halt. By May 2003 the unemployment rate in the Magic Valley adjusted to 3.5 percent; in the nation, 6.1 percent.

Downtown Revitalization Meant Success

Compensation for historic remodeling and restoring of BID (Business Improvement District) property was made available after the City Council approved the guidelines written by the Twin Falls City Historic Preservation Commission. Properties on the National Register of Historic Places would get 20 percent tax credit; owners of properties not on the Register could apply for funds from URA's Rehab Financing Program.

Taking advantage of the tax credit was lawyer Jeff Hepworth, owner of the registered Gem State Paper Building on Second Street S, which was built in 1916 as the Simpson Warehouse. The URA participated with Hepworth's Simpson and Company in the $1.6 million renovation of the building for professional offices by providing a 35-car parking lot behind the structure on Sande's lot. Meanwhile, the URA removed several "junk buildings" in the Twin Falls Historic Warehouse District and cleared the lots in preparation for future commercial/residential—not industrial—development.

Twin Falls is considered by the National Trust for Historic Preservation in San Francisco to be the most successful of all Carey Act projects in the United States.
—Paul Smith (2001)

The City of Twin Falls undertook the largest National Register nomination ever listed in the State of Idaho. The Twin Falls Original Townsite Residential Historic District National Register nomination contains 929 properties and was accepted by the Keeper of the National Register on November 30, 2001.
—The Idaho State Historical Society (2002)

The Urban Renewal Agency—almost broke due to its help in getting Dell established—continued to upgrade Historic Downtown with a new sprinkler system and the replacement of diseased trees. There, some changes, restorations, and turnovers occurred. Early in 2002 Ken Edmonds and Gus Bowman purchased the 1940 Radio Rondevoo (Calvary Chapel, 1983–2000) and restored it as a community center for dances, concerts, and sports events. Tom Ashenbrener discontinued his hardware department, expanded the housewares department, and gave Price Hardware a new name: Rudy's, A Cook's Paradise.

We'll continue to operate under the ideals Father instilled in us: respect for our customers and knowledge of what we sell.
—Tom Ashenbrener

Historical Update: One of the stores constructed in 1904 was not known until 2003 when Ashenbrener undertook to restore his building at 147 Main Avenue W. Under the old façade was a lovely red brick front imbedded with a concrete plaque that read "Messer Block 1904." So, not only does Rudy's (Price Hardware) claim to be the oldest retail store in Twin Falls, it is also in one of the two known oldest buildings in town. The old 1904 red bricks were so crumbly, Tom had them replaced immediately keeping the original design and color. The same was done for the old yellow bricks on his building next door.

Those historic buildings are what this town is all about.
—Al Zelinka, RFB Consulting of Irvine, California

Hudson's Shoes, opened by Voy Hudson in 1930, closed its store in the Booth Building on Main Avenue S but retained its Lynwood store. The vacated store was filled by Lillis Anderson and Kelly Wren's A Pleasant Surprise, a gift shop that featured local artists and companies. Christina's Women's Clothing closed and was replaced by Bill and Diane Workman's Cobble Creek Clothier. The owners of two excellent downtown restaurants, Mark Matin of A'Roma and Greg Smith of Mama Inez, pooled their culinary expertise, moved together to The Royal in the Campus Mall on Filer Avenue, and opened a new restaurant, Señor Caesar. Peach Tree Creek Restaurant filled the Mama Inez vacancy, and South Pacific Grill filled the void left by Uptown Bistro in the Harder Building.

In April 2003 Magic Valley Bank consolidated its three branches into one and moved into the vacated Wells Fargo Building on the corner of Main and Shoshone W. The Perrine Partnership, LLC, directors of the Magic Valley Bank, purchased that building on the site of the 1905 Perrine Hotel. With a focus on history and help from the URA, the partners remodeled the exterior to bring the structure more in line with the architectural patterns of Twin Falls early days.

The City's Business Became More Complex

Twin Falls government saw two new records in 2000: Councilman Elaine Steele became Twin Falls's first woman mayor, chosen by a seven-member City Council, three of whom were women—another record. Gloria Galan was the first Hispanic to run for city council in twenty-five years. The man who was first to run, lost; Galan won her seat on the council. Galan was also a member of the National Advisory Council on Migrant Health from 1998 to 2002. In 2001 councilman Chris Talkington was appointed director of the Snake River Juvenile Detention Center where his program included a greater push to hold adults responsible and a mediation program in which the juvenile offenders must meet in person with their victims and work out payment plans for restitution.

While the 2000 census showed that the population of Twin Falls had grown to thirty-five thousand, the nine (add Elmore) Magic Valley counties plus northern Nevada gave Twin Falls a trade-and-services census of 200,000. Washington Street was widened to four lanes north to Falls Avenue. Recreation fees went up 5 percent to cover city employees' first raise in ten years. Wal-Mart's request for zoning and PUD (Planned Unit Development) changes was denied, and another huge subdivision gained approval only after the developer modified his plans to address concerns of neighbors.

> *Some day Falls Avenue will be four lanes. . . . A second bridge* [over the Snake River] *is at least twenty-five years away.*
>
> —Trip R. Craig, city councilman (2002)

When Lance Clow was chosen mayor in 2002, sitting on the City Council were three ex-mayors: Elaine Steele, vice mayor; Howard Allen, and Chris Talkington. Twin Falls voters passed a $500,000 tax-override bond (a Twin Falls first) to help purchase the vacated Treasure Cove Building on Shoshone Street W for a new Senior Center, where volunteers donated labor worth $150,000.

In September 2002 Twin Falls became the first city in Idaho with "311" phone-dialing service for non-emergencies. Community service officers at the non-emergency call center syphoned much of the report-taking and paperwork away from street officers. The result in the first three months of 2003 was the reduction of the Twin Falls Police Department's entire load by 45 percent. The street officers' freed-up time was directed toward more active crime prevention and more aggressive narcotics detection and enforcement. Added to the department's bomb squad was a $128,500 robot to help in SWAT operations and in explosives and hazard materials handling. Twin Falls's squad was one of only four nationally accredited bomb squads in the state.

The 1989 County Jail with 220 beds was chronically overcrowded, but a $16 million bond issue was rejected in May 2002. The County Commissioners would consider a suggestion from a citizens committee to have a private company build a new jail that the county could buy back through a lease program. The committee proposed building with the $400,000 being spent each year to house prisoners in other counties, eliminating the need for a bond election.

Late in 2002, the new city council chambers opened in a brick building that the city purchased at 305 Third Avenue E, across from City Hall. The new chambers boasted four thousand square feet (three times larger than the old 1952 chambers), a digital overhead projector, and wiring to take advantage of modern fiber optics technology. With interior design by City Hall architect Harald Gerber, the building included city offices and conference rooms.

In 2003 the rough intersection at the corner of Main and Shoshone was enhanced with a pattern of stamped concrete pavement in red and tan, which replaced the thirty-year-old brick circle, plus new crosswalks and two decorative streetlights. At the prodding of downtown businessmen—who thought the street numbering system was shopper-unfriendly—the City Council agreed to have the street names in the townsite changed from numbers to place-names in alphabetical order starting at the northwest corner.

> *The streets are quirky. These names are quirky, but they are a new quirky.* —Chris Talkington, city councilman (2003)

To Consolidate or Not to Consolidate

In January 2002 Magic Valley Regional Medical Center (MVRMC) bought the privately-owned Twin Falls Clinic and Hospital, which became the MVRMC "downtown campus." With the Clinic no longer private property, the county tax rolls were reduced by the loss of a $3 million evaluation. The Clinic's emergency room closed, as did the Professional Pharmacy after fifty-five years. MVRMC made another move that year. For more than twenty years, St. Luke's Mountain States Tumor Institute (MSTI) had provided cancer services in the Magic Valley. MVRMC leased its ten-year-old cancer center at 656 Addison West to St. Luke's MSTI with a 40/60 percent share in profits and losses because of the difficulty of recruiting oncologists to rural Twin Falls County.

> *Even though these facilities no longer exist as separate entities, the quality of health care continues under one umbrella.*
> —Shawn Barigar, public relations coordinator, MVRMC (2003)

Schools Balked at Consolidation. The last time was in 1948 when the state's one thousand school districts were combined to form one hundred districts; other attempts at consolidation were in 1986 and 1994. In 2002 the state had 114 districts showing a trend toward deconsolidation. Magic Valley had twenty-two separate districts, most with less than one thousand students, each with its own school board and superintendent.

> *Asking residents of a school district to consolidate with another district is more than asking them to share administrative services; it's asking them to give up their very identity. . . . In nearly every town across the Magic Valley the public school acts as the heart and soul of the community.* —Robert Mayer, *The Times-News* staff

With the state's $200 million budget shortfall, numerous local positions were eliminated: twelve teachers, the audiologist, administrators, and classified personnel.

> *Federal mandates and state accountability directives are imposing an ever increasing burden upon the district, and the "bar" for student performance is being raised higher and higher.*
>
> —Terrell Donicht, superintendent,
> Twin Falls School District #411, until June 2003

Yet, Twin Falls schools did so much on so little. In 2002 the average SAT (Standard Achievement Test) and ACT scores for Twin Falls High School students were above those of Idaho and the nation. The Twin Falls School District received the *Blue Ribbon* award for the third year placing this district in the top one-third of districts in the nation in terms of employability of it graduates. Twelve Twin Falls teachers and one district administrator achieved National Board Certification after completing a rigorous program.

Honors Celebrated Twin Falls Traditions

Bridge No. 17580 became officially the Perrine Bridge on 4 April 2000 when Gov. Dirk Kempthorne signed Rep. Leon Smith's bill, which passed the Senate 35–0. Former-governor Cecil Andrus, who obtained emergency federal funds to completely finance the new bridge in 1974, said "it has always been the Perrine Bridge. It was named the Perrine Bridge by choice of the people."

The memory of another pioneer was honored at the funeral of Claude Brown Jr. who died in 2000 at the age of eighty-two. Claude Jr. had managed the drapery department of Claude Brown's Home Furnishings which his father, who died in 1952, founded in 1919. Like Sam Hamilton and Gus Kelker in the decades before him, Claude Jr. was a prankster and "the funniest man in town." He organized the Kiwanis's popcorn sales in City Park during summer band concerts and sold "Claude's Corn" for many years before his health began to fail. At Claude Jr.'s funeral the eulogy was given by his long-time friend Roy Babbel, age eighty-six, and the prayer by Jack Frederickson, age ninety-one.

Burt Huish became a one-man Twin Falls tradition. From 1994 to 2002, Huish sang *The Star Spangled Banner* 44 times before 21 of the 30 major league baseball games in 21 big league parks. In the beginning of 2003 he sang at three major league games and had two more lined up. Between 1999 and 2004 Burt sang for 12 NBA Jazz games. In April 2003 Burt sang in Boise when that city won the World Cup Wrestling Match.

Commitment to a healthy environment for employees and patrons became a tradition in Twin Falls, and honors went to three locals. Ken and Laura Schmidt, the owners of La Casita Mexican Restaurant who started their no-smoking policy in 1993, were honored for their commitment by two anti-tobacco groups. Lisa Buddecke, who started the Magic Valley Drug-free Workplace Project in 1997, was honored by being nominated "2002 Chamber Person of the Year" by the Chamber of Commerce. With the support of six drug-free businesses, Lisa applied her experience in insurance marketing to her project. By 2003, eighty-nine Magic Valley businesses and organizations representing 7,519 employees were program members.

Beautification became another Twin Falls tradition when Rex Lytle became the chairman of the Beautification Committee of the Chamber of Commerce. The committee came up with a new contest in 2001 to award the dressing-up of industrial areas: Landscape Excellence Awards to one large and one small company. Seastrom Manufacturing and the Twin Falls Canal Company were honored with plaques that year.

The Olympics Committee of the 2002 Winter Olympics, which were held in Salt Lake City, Utah, honored Twin Falls by selecting it to be one of the smallest towns along the route to host torch relay runners—forty-five of them. Among the relay runners were Curtis H. Eaton representing "the Heart of the Community," Tom Courtney representing the City as its manager, and Jan Mittleider, health education professor at CSI, who represented her Over 60 and Getting Fit class.

> *Organizers from Utah* [said] *they felt more welcome in Twin Falls than anywhere else.*
> —Mayor Elaine Steele, chairman,
> Twin Falls Olympic Torch Relay Committee

Steele was honored by the Chamber of Commerce who named her 2002 Chamber Person of the Year along with Randy Hansen who helped organize the events for the Torch Relay. Lifetime Achievement awards went to Curtis H. Eaton and CSI President Jerry Meyerhoeffer.

From Honors to Scandals, Not a Tradition. In its first one hundred years Twin Falls was quite free of scandals, which are often a sign of the times. Certainly a sign of the times in 1919 was the scandalization of all of Idaho when Washington Elementary School teacher Juanita Dean admitted that she was married. A sign of the times in 2002 was the confession of Bickel Elementary School Principal Mary Lee Roberts to the possession of a controlled substance: Roberts had mailed a package containing about a pound of marijuana from Texas to her Twin Falls home. She resigned shortly after the felony charge—of possessing more than three ounces of the substance—was filed against her. Roberts entered a Drug Court program and was kicked out of it in June 2003, sending her back to the regular judicial system. She may be placed on probation, sentenced to prison, or to do community service.

Another sign of the times appeared at the Twin Falls Public Library. Cybersitter software, which blocks sexually explicit Web sites, was installed on two of the many computers in the main room and on all computers in the children's section.

Park Systems Continued to Expand

By 2003, Twin Falls City Parks Department properties consisted of eight hundred acres in twenty-eight public areas including parks, playgrounds, ball fields, swimming pool, recreation facilities, parking lots, and trail systems. The 8.5-acre Vista Bonita Park was created on the south side of Twin Falls in 2000 with a pressure irrigation system, rest rooms, picnic shelter, volleyball and basketball courts, playground, walking trails . . . and trees. Cub Scout Packs No. 60 and No. 104 planted three of the seven trees, and

Boy Scout Troops No. 67 and No. 90, assisting with an Eagle Scout project in 2002, dug holes for thirty-four trees that were donated by the Idaho Power Company and through a grant from the Idaho Department of Lands. On three acres donated by Devoe Brown, Jason's Woodland Hills Park brought the number of city parks to seventeen in 2001. That year Harmon Park got a 10,000-square-foot skate park.

On Arbor Day 2002 forty volunteers of the Key Club, sponsored by the Kiwanis Club, and the Tree Commission planted eight trees in City Park to replace ten that were removed as damaged, diseased, or dangerous—some believed to have been planted in 1904 by James A. Waters. Three of the new plantings were cherry trees to commemorate the Minidoka Relocation "Hunt Camp." Also that year, City Pool budget was in the red, and the City contracted with the YMCA to manage the pool: City to pay for maintenance, Y to pay the personnel.

With city access to state- and private-owned land, the Snake River Canyon Rim Trail was extended eastward from the Visitor Center parking lot, went under the Perrine Bridge, then another three-quarters of a mile with four great canyon views, to just below Pillar Falls. The Rim Trail, in two sections, then totaled one and a quarter miles. The Perrine Bridge became one of two bridges in the nation to host an association of from forty to sixty BASE (Buildings, Antennae, Spans, Earth) jumpers annually. Jumping at the bridge in West Virginia was limited to one week a year; Perrine Bridge was open to BASE jumpers all year, every day.

Construction began in 2001 on the five-year improvement project at Shoshone Falls Park with replacement of the overlook platform and a new, wider staircase, bigger parking lot, and new restrooms. Dierkes Lake got an enlarged double swim area. In 2003 the City Council diverted some Idaho Power money toward rebuilding the old stagecoach road up and out of the Snake River Canyon near Shoshone Falls Park in time for the city's centennial celebration. Twin Falls purchased 545 acres at Auger Falls to preserve as a park for $1.3 million from the city's reserve funds; volunteers would help with restoration of the "Auger Falls Urban Wilderness."

Twin Falls County received a grant from the Idaho Department of Parks and Recreation for a campground at Rock Creek Park. The 1916 Curry School Building that houses the Twin Falls County Historical Society

Museum, not far from Rock Creek Park on West Addison Avenue, was placed on the National Register and became a Visitor Center in 2002. A new soccer complex on forty acres of farmland just west of the city would be ready in the fall of 2004 with twelve full-sized soccer fields and a 5-acre parking lot.

The state of Idaho bought two unconnected properties totaling 281 acres to add Billingsley Creek State Park to its other six parks along the Middle Snake River: Niagara Springs, Crystal Springs, Blue Heart Springs, Minnie Miller Springs, Malad Gorge, and Box Canyon. Idaho was one of thirty-one states where wildlife watching brought in more cash than hunting and fishing—a dramatic shift in outdoor emphasis since 1969, but which had been building for twenty years.

As President Clinton prepared to leave office, his executive order expanded the Craters of the Moon National Monument (established in 1924) from 54,000 acres to 754,000 acres of volcanic craters, cones, lava flows, caves, and fissures of the 65-mile-long Great Rift, one of the longest and deepest on Earth. Craters would be administered jointly by NPS and BLM. In January 2001, Congress created the 73-acre Minidoka Internment National Monument, also to be administered by Hagerman Fossil Beds N.M.

THE MINIDOKA MONUMENT
ENTRANCE STATION AND WAITING ROOM, 2002

Water, Ever Critical

The Twin Falls canal system turned ninety-five years old in 2000. Back in 1905, water began its flow from the new Milner Dam into the southside canals. In 1921 we saw Charles Stephens ride endless canal banks in a dusty pickup truck checking water levels and changing settings on control gates. By 2000, ditch riders and water masters depended on cell phones and new computerized controls that maintained desired water levels throughout most of the system and could be monitored and adjusted by a computer in the office.

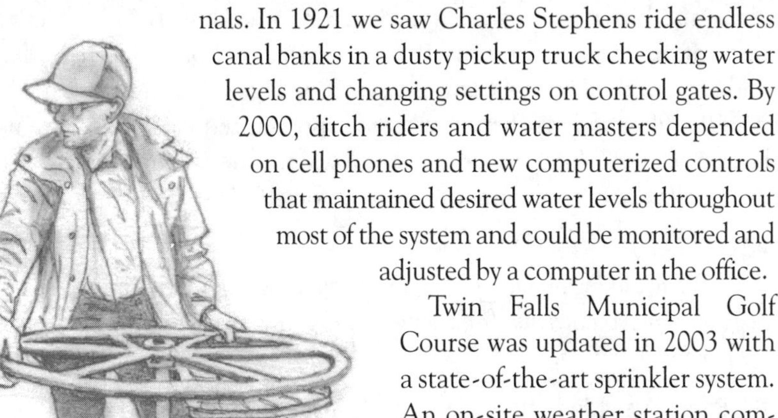

WATERMASTER

Twin Falls Municipal Golf Course was updated in 2003 with a state-of-the-art sprinkler system. An on-site weather station computed grass moisture conditions which were then adjusted by keycode and relayed by radio over a satellite network installed around the grounds. In less than ten seconds, over six hundred sprinklers were dousing as directed.

> *Until 1976, flood irrigation was used—flooded like a lake on Monday, dry as a bone by Sunday. Then the hydraulic-based system that was installed became outdated.*—Mike Hamblin, course manager (2003)

Strides Were Made in Water Pollution Control. Under the Clean Water Act, a federal judge in 1995 gave Idaho five years to produce cleanup plans for 962 polluted streams. Two years later, the Twin Falls Canal Company had thirty settling ponds to trap sediment in irrigation flows and keep soil on the land rather than going into the Snake River. By pooling its resources with several state agencies to build a series of settling ponds, the Canal Company had one hundred ponds by 2001. The results were dramatic.

Equally impressive was the change in sediment level of Rock Creek as it drained and irrigated about 200,000 acres of forest, rangeland, and farmland. Sonny Buhidar, water quality analyst for the Department of Environmental Quality (DEQ), looked beyond the gains made in controlling soil runoff to the non-point pollution from all farm runoff.

It's going to be a while before Rock Creek meets water quality standards.
—Sonny Buhidar (2001)

The City Council mandated that all city subdivisions were to use the pressurized irrigation system for landscape watering. Twin Falls entered a restoration project along the Perrine Coulee and on a dozen wetlands in and around the city to be started by 2005. This would improve habitat for wildlife, filter sediment from water for pressurized irrigation systems, and boost the city's ability to handle storm water runoff. Twin Falls County and Twin Falls Canal Company were also involved; the U.S. Army Corps of Engineers would do the work.

We're talking about building some wetlands that we can put crops on to remove nutrients from some of the canal water that runs through here.
—Gary Young, city engineer

An Effort Was Made to Protect and Conserve Drinking Water. The main source of water for some 200,000 people in southern Idaho is the Snake River Aquifer. In December 2002 the EPA fined the Energy Department $175,000 for failing to take steps to keep radioactive material in soils at INEEL (Idaho National Environmental and Engineering Lab) from leaching into that aquifer. In 2003 the Southwest Irrigation District planned for aquifer conservation with incentives for farmers to refrain from pumping water for irrigation to help maintain the groundwater level.

There's no question that we're mining water. We are going to pay for this thing sooner or later.
—Paul Christensen, Cassia County commissioner

Also that year, Twin Falls City Council purchased ninety-three acres of property near the Washington Street well for future recharge of that aquifer from which the city draws its drinking water.

On the campus of the College of Southern Idaho (CSI), a surface irrigation system reduced use of city well water by 10 percent. CSI expected eventually to rely completely on surface irrigation for its 240-acre campus plus the 140 acres of its north campus (. . . the way Twin Falls relied on surface irrigation starting in 1904; some of the original little irrigation ditches are still seen, and used, in many parts of town today). Ten years earlier, in 1992, two organic gardeners, Rose Garber and Steve Tanguy, started the Twin Falls Farmers' Market in the K-Mart parking lot. In 2002 Rose and

Steve retired and the market moved to the CSI north campus, the college's Breckenridge Ag Endowment Farm. To complement the market's new location, the college's horticulture and plant-science faculty and students laid out a community garden. Citizens signed up for 25-by-50-foot plots and raised their own produce to consume and/or sell at the nearby Twin Falls Farmers' Market.

Agriculture and Twin Falls Came Full Circle in 100 Years

On the larger scale, farming in the Magic Valley saw cost efficiency through computer guidance for such operations as data mapping, sprinkler pivoting, fuel mixture regulation, and seed distribution. Increased yield came through GPS (Global Positioning System) technology, which helped with such operations as fertilizer dispensing and application. With a laptop or pocket computer a farmer could diagnose his problems through a code program as well as keep his farm books. The trend was toward fewer farmers.

Large family (corporate) farms competed globally, but in the long run, their experience would probably not be similar to the other globalized Twin Falls businesses. Environmental laws applied to crop lands of large acreage, and enforcement made management costly. Thus, management of the lands of small acreage, with minimal environmental impact, was freed up to diversify into specialty seeds crops, organically certified seed varieties, wind-generated power plants, ethanol plants, and conservation easements that left land open for recreation and aesthetics. Small acreages were also put into crops to sell to neighbors and at local markets. Consumers began to care about where their food came from and bought locally grown food.

Along with very large agribusiness (tens of thousands of acres), family farming today and in the future will resemble small farms and local markets of the past. —Robert Lowder, professor of agriculture, CSI

While Twin Falls's economic base continued to be agriculture, the city made a gradual transition—with the help of Business Plus I, II, and III—into a diversified economy adding retail, commerce, and light industry to the base. And so, starting with I. B. Perrine's irrigation project as "Business Plus Zero," and adding all the contributions of pioneers old and new, Twin Falls's first one hundred years were accomplished in a way that would have pleased Bert Perrine, Father of Twin Falls.

The *Mission Statement for the City of Twin Falls*, which was written by the 1994 City Council and remained unchanged by the four succeeding councils, forms an inspirational base for the town's second one hundred years:

Our mission, as stewards of the public trust, is to meet the current and future needs of the community, promote citizen involvement, preserve our heritage, protect our social and physical resources, and enhance the quality of life in Twin Falls.

General Index

Subject Index